An Introduction FOR OUR PICTORIAL AND GRAPHIC VIEW OF

CENTURY-OLD TRENTON

This centennial history has been prepared in response to a general demand for a souvenir booklet commemorating the one hundredth birthday of Trenton, Missouri.

While not intended primarily as a history reference, nevertheless it contains, to the best of knowledge of its contributors, a true and accurate record of our town structurally and economically, recording in pictures and story some of the old, some of the new.

Needless to say there remains none among us who can remember back to Trenton's beginning. For this early data the committee referred to three existing histories of Grundy County: Birdsall & Dean 1881, James Everett Ford 1908, and William R. Denslow 1939. The committee is especially grateful for the advice and pictures furnished by Ray V. Denslow, and for the generosity of William R. Denslow in permitting a liberal use of material in his history. For those desiring a more comprehensive history of Trenton and Grundy County, it is recommended that they secure a copy of Mr. Denslow's book.

To record for later generations, the industries, merchants and professional people of Trenton have contributed funds to provide the advertising contained herein which not only financed a major portion of this book but also gave us a printed record of the Trenton we know today.

It is also desired to acknowledge the valuable assistance of Frank Kirkman in the handling of advertising copy and of Charles D. Gipson in securing and identifying old pictures. Also, a special tribute is made to Glen Drinkard, who furnished pictures and assisted in securing historical data prior to his untimely passing.

The following residents have been liberal in lending the committee many pictures of early industry, of pioneers and of buildings long since moved or demolished to make way for progress: Miss Lucy Crooks, Jim Collier, Charles McCallum, Alice Dye, Albert Burress, Kemp Scott, Jess Turner, Jerrold Stuart, Wilbur Austin, Marie Hatfield, Harvey Hudson, W. Klingingsmith, Mrs. Ora Clingingsmith, Mrs. Jess Bryant, Mrs. Delmar Sharp, Ross McClintic, Harry Witten, F. G. Lehew, Fred G. Thomas, Mrs. Harry Asher, Mrs. Rose Russell, Helen Doty, James O. Robinson, R. S. Hatfield, Mrs. John Layson, W. W. Alexander, Charles Skinner, Floyd Pew and Mrs. Roy Hulen. Unfortunately, due to lack of space, some excellent pictures could not be shown in the book.

The sections on church history were edited by Tom Brown, teacher at Trenton High School. He was assisted in this work by the following students: Rev. Stewart Whitney, Beverley Moore, Karen Pollard, Paul Boysal, John Caldwell, Linda Blackmore, Linda Chapin, Sandra Buzzard, Nancy Ball, Anita Good, Janet Ross, Barbara Lame, Harry Dryer, Joyce Hann, C; rl Guenther, Orenda Trumbo. The Republican Times and Station KTTN were especially helpful in securing pictures for the history section.

Accordingly, your committee gratefully places in your hands this book in the hope, if you are a former resident, that it may be a lasting record of your return "back home". If you are a resident, it will give you a better perspective of what may have heretofore gone unnoticed in your work-a-day life.

Eric Sonnich, Chairman
Trenton Centennial History Committee

OUR CENTENNIAL MAYOR J. H. COOK

Many stories have been told, retold, exaggerated or forgotten in the past century of life in Trenton. There are many incidents, which will never be recalled, having been lost in the retelling or modified by official records.

This book is not intended to be a comprehensive history, but rather a Centennial Book - to recall the past and record the present. It is published in a spirit of Centennial Times - a festival spirit, and in celebrating the passing of one hundred years since Trenton was founded, its citizens look to the future in the hope that those who follow will treasure our heritage and add their contribution to the story of a good and thoroughly American town.

J. H. Cook, Mayor

The following civic minded citizens of Trenton, having confidence in the community and its ability to co-operate in a successful centennial have each advanced the sum of $100.00 as a loan to the Trenton Centennial Committee in order that this committee might be able to produce the finest type of centennial celebration. The complete support of our people will assure these citizens that their confidence is well reposed. J. H. Cook, E. Knudsen, Tad A. Simons, Cisco-Brown Drug Store, Pickett, Andereck & Hauck, Trenton National Bank by R. E. Cullers, Dale and Bach Jewelry Company, Republican Times, Trenton Trust Company, Hotel Plaza, R. Leroy Miller, Nisbeth Chevrolet Company, Grand River Press, Trenton Hardware, Herb Brown, Mart Drug #2, C. L. Clark, M. D., Donoho's, Gipson Furniture Company, Central Farm Products Company, G. H. McCullough, McVay Motor Company, Gardner-Skinner, Hoffman-Reed, Bock Truck & Tractor Company, Hy-Vee Food Store, Boehner's IGA Super Market, Dean N. Bogue, The Gables, Service Laundry & Cleaners, D.• H. Mason, George Stone, Bones Lionberger, Home Gas & Appliance Corp., R. D. Krehbiel, Helmandollar Motor Co., Ray C. Denslow, KTTN, Frank E. Lafferty, J. C. Penney Co., Muffs Bakery, Julian Pyatt, Nathan Stein, Ellis & Bullock, Dr. Oliver Duffy, Reed & Whisler Jewelry, Fair Drug Company, Muriel Davis Food Store, Bert Hoover, Henry Goodin, Hy-Power Oil Company, Galen W. Nielsen, Grundy Co. Lumber Co., Davis-Black more, Missouri Public Service Co., Bond Wholesale, Montgomery Ward & Co.

A Century Ago

The hardships of the pioneers can hardly be appreciated or understood by those of us who live in another age. The modern tramp would shun the "home" of those years. Round logs, notched on the ends, formed the sides of the small cabin which was usually a story and a half structure with a thatched roof. A loft was used for storage space or for an extra bed, if a little hay was thrown in the corner. Sometimes the floor was dirt, but the more ambitious split logs with the split surface to serve as the floor. Mud filled in the large spaces left by the ill-fitting logs and the fireplace, used for heating and cooking, was constructed of mud and sticks. Weighted poles kept the roof from blowing away on a stormy night. The windows were covered with oilcloth, or thinly scraped and oiled skins in the winter, and left open in the warmer weather. Sometimes a remo%,able log served the purpose, and some cabins had no windows at all. The raising of a cabin in the neighborhood was accomplished with the assistance of the families for miles around and 15 or 20 men would complete it in a day. The trimming of the protruding ends, cutting the windows, laying the floor and building the fireplace was left for the owner to attend to at his earliest convenience.

Where we run down to the corner store for a sack of flour, the early settler took a week off to make a hundred-mile journey to the river towns of Brunswick or Lexington and brought back supplies for the neighborhood. The next trip was made by another neighbor. Even when the first store was established by Lomax and Jacobs in Bluff Grove (now Trenton), it was a two-day trip for the residents of the outlying settlements.

The first store house was erected by Daniel Devaul with the assistance of his son, James R. It was a fine building for those days. Generally the cabins were built of round logs, but in the new store, the logs were all hewn square and nicely fitted, while the plastering was done with real lime mortar instead of mud. It was located at Bluff Grove on what was later known as the Ridgeway property, probably near the vicinity of Ridgeway and 7th street. On a visit to Richmond, Ray county, in 1838, Devaul persuaded James I. Lomax and his brother-in-law, Thomas Jacobs, to bring a stock of goods to the settlement and open a store, agreeing to rent the log palace to them for a place of business. Accepting the offer, they opened the first store in Grundy county. The settlement up to that time had been called Moore's, or Moore's Settlement, but from the oaerdrig of the store, it was known as Lomax's Store, as well as the Bluffs or Bluff Grove.

Lomax and Jacobs did not long have a monopoly in the mercantile business for William Thrailkill & Brother opened a store the following year and they were followed by James L. Henshaw, the latter's store being located not far from the Lomax establishment on the Ridgeway property. Some of the logs hewn by Daniel Devaul for the Lomax store did service for a hundred years in the old Hume house on 7th street which was torn down about 1937.

Before the opening of Lomax's store, the farmers loaded their wagons with skins of all kinds, such as deer, coon, mink, muskrat, with venison, hams and honey and departed for the river towns of Brunswick, Glasgow, Richmond and Lexington, returning with their winter supply of groceries, flour and whisky. Lomax hauled his goods from Richmond with ox wagons. Goods were hauled in those days from Glasgow at 60 cents a hundred pounds.

The first horse mill was set up by James Bunch in 1836. The customer furnished his own horsepower and Bunch collected one-eighth as toll.

In the Center
Of The Scene ...

100 Years Ago

One hundred years is a long time. Four generations, in reality, are represented in that span of a century.

Stories of Indian raids and wagon trains are so remote to today's resident that they seem more like legends and folklore than actual happenings that took place right in Grundy county - in Trenton, Missouri.

To our parents, our grandparents and those before them, it is only a step backward to that time one hundred years ago when Trenton had its beginning.

Until November 16, 1820, the territory now embraced by Grundy county formed a part of Howard county; after this date, it became a part of Ray county until January 2, 1833, when it was attached to the newly organized Carroll county. When the metes and bounds of Livingston county were set forth and Gov. Dunklin approved the creation of that county on January 6, 1837, the last paragraph contained the following provision:

"All that territory lying north of said county of Livingston shall be attached to said county for all civil and military purposes until otherwise provided by law."

As it can be seen, this not only included the present territory of Grundy, but Mercer county, too. At the first meeting of the county court of Livingston, the judges, who were William Martin, Joseph Cox and Reuben McCoskrie, inscribed the following order (April 7, 1837):

"By order of court all the territory north of Livingston county is to be divided into two townships. All east of the East fork be known by the name of Muddy Creek township, all west of the East fork be known as Sugar Creek township."

At this term, the first election to be held in Grundy county was ordered for May 27, 1837. In Sugar Creek township, the election was held in the home of George Peery, the election judges being William P. Thompson, George Bunch and Philip Wild. The Muddy Creek election took place in Daniel Devaul's home and the judges were John Thrailkill, Daniel Devaul and William S. Cochran. Little interest was manifested in the Grundy territory until February, 1838, when William P. Thompson of Sugar Creek township was one of the three judges elected to compose the county court of Livingston county and upon meeting of the court, was made presiding justice by motion of David H. Dunkerson, one of his associate justices. He held the position up to, and including, the February term, 1841, when Grundy county was organized, his residence being located therein. He was the first clerk of Grundy county and one of the first justices of the county court of Ray county.

The county of Grundy was named after the Hon. Felix Grundy, attorney general of the United States under President Andrew Jackson. It was logical to name a territory settled by immigrants from Tennessee after an honored citizen of that state. Grundy died almost exactly a year before the county honored his name.

The bill organizing the county was brought before the legislature early in January, but it was not approved until January 29, 1841; thus, while sections thirteen, fourteen and fifteen, making Grundy a county, were passed by the legislature, January 2, 1841, the bill was not completed for several days after and did not become a law until approved January 29, 1841.

On the same day Gov. Thomas Reynolds appointed William Thrailkill as the first sheriff of the county. The territory embraced by the act of legislature forms almost a perfect square, the north and south distance being twenty and one-half miles and the east and west distance, twenty-one miles, the total acreage being 273,357.39.

Early Settlers

James R. Merrill one of the early settlers of Trenton, and a prominent citizen of Grundy county came to Grundy county in 1837 and invested in land in different parts of the county. His homestead then adjoined Trenton but is now a part of the city, known as Merrill's addition. At the organization of the county in 1841, he was appointed the first treasurer, he held until 1846. In 1850, he was elected county judge. Mrs. Harry L. Asher of Trenton, is his grandaughter. He was the second Master of Trenton Lodge No. 111, A.F. & A. M. and served from 1852-1854.

Following W. P. Thompson, in the spring of 1834, came "Uncle" Levi Moore and his large family, who were the first settlers east of the river, locating on the present site of Trenton. Besides his numerous children, his four sons-in-law, William Cochran, John Thrailkill, George Tetherow and Yancy Stokes, accompanied Moore from Randolph and Howard counties. William Thrailkill was the first sheriff of the county and John Thrailkill, one of the first election judges. Uncle Levi died in 1875, at the age of 100, a lively and jovial character whose tales of pioneer life made him the center of attraction with young folks. His farm became known as the Lomax and Jacob land.

In the Edinburg neighborhood settled George Peery and his sons, William, Archibald, and a daughter, Louisa. Jewett Norris, donor of the library, arrived, too. Evans Peery, his son, William N., and George Peery settled on the west side of the river. Daniel Devaul came in March, 1835, bringing a wife and eight children. He first settled near the river on the east side, known as the Old Benson tract, but in 1838 sold his claim to Samuel Benson. Devaul was a man of great energy and character, and with the assistance of his son, James R. Devaul, built the first store in Grundy county. Devaul left for California in the gold rush of '49, prospected in Nevada, and eventually settled near San Jose, Cal. , where he died in 1871.

At the close of 1835, there was only a sprinkling of settlers in the county, located mainly around the present town of Trenton (then Moore's settlement); in Madison township, northeast of "Buck Snort", or Edinburg; and in the Lindley settlement to the southeast. The cabins were few and far between and the residents would go for weeks at a time without seeing a sign of a human, except their own family. With few exceptions, the settlers in this area immigrated from the states of Virginia, Kentucky, Tennessee and Ohio, as in those days river travel was the only practical way to move an entire family and its belongings.

The years of 1836-38 saw heavy immigration. Down the Ohio, up the Mississippi, Missouri and Grand rivers they came. Usually in parties of five to fifteen families each, generally settling in the same neighborhood, forming a company of old time acquaintances. In 1836 and 1837, the government surveyed this portion of the state, opening a government land office at Lexington in 1839. This was the beginning of the real influx of settlers to Grundy county. They loaded their wagons with the currency of the time, including skins venison, beeswax and honey, and sold them at the river markets for the precious silver with which to purchase their claims. The speculators bought heavily--and lost heavily, for the opening of the Platte Purchase in 1837 diverted many of the settlers from the Grand river valley into the area west of here.

In the fall of 1837, the Bain settlement sprang up in Lincoln township, east of the present village of Tindall. It was composed of Jesse and Riason Bain, Samuel Kelso, Henry Foster and William Dille. At this time it was the most northerly location in the county. On the west side of the river, William McCammon, William Metcalf, Elisha Inman, the Oxfords, Grubbs, Applegates and Winns made their homes.

The years of 1838-39 brought the Merrills, Landys, Houstons, Townsends and George McCready, all originally from Maryland. James Weldon came this year. Thomas N. Carnes, the Kirkendalls, Stokes', Moores, Cochrans and Woods arrived in the spring of '38, along with the Schoolers, Renfros, Collins, Rooks, Holloways, Lydas, Drinkards, Spears, Winters, Andersons, Perkins, Chrismans, Larkin Fields, John and Jethro Sires, Robert Hobbs, John McHargue, John Priest and the Ashbrooks. The Warrens, Kilburns and Merrimans settled Wilson township in 1839.

CENTENNIAL GREETINGS

NEW

OLD

ROCK ISLAND LINES

Farm Life 100 Years Ago. .

A STRIKING CONTRAST TO THAT OF 1957

The pioneer farmers of Grundy county displayed courage supreme and endurance almost unbelieveable to clear land and establish those first farms. They were a self-sustaining group of resourceful men and women who improvised for practically all their needs.

Those few scattered farms of 100 years ago were unpretentious as contrasted to the modern Taylor county farm. The typical pioneer farm home was furnished primarily with "homemade" furniture. The more prosperous tiller of the soil had a pot bellied stove and a wood burning range; but many others were content with an open fireplace for heating and cooking. On the floors, if they had any covering at all, were rag rugs padded with straw. "Body-rest" mattresses were made of feathers or straw placed on a crude but sturdy bed without springs.

Those first farmers of this area depended on horses and cattle raised on their farms for their farm power. Horses and cattle were also used to transport products to market. Some of those enterprising farmers used dogs, sheep, or goats to "power" the tread mills for pumping water or for similar tasks. It was many years before the steam engine was available as power for the threshing crew. The pioneer farmer of Grundy county was "born 70 years too soon" to reap the benefits of the row crop tractor that gave agriculture its biggest revolutionary change about 1930.

PETTERSON'S THRESHING CREW

The 1957 farmer is using the most up-to-date machinery, tractors, cultivators and corn pickers, which were unknown to the 'back-breaking' pioneer farmer. Many of today's Centennial observers can remember when the threshing machine was discarded for combine and when the corn picker was first perfected.

BIG SCALE COMBINING

Wm. Gipson

Charles D. Gipson

Charles W. Gipson

Gipson Furniture Co.
AND
Gipson Funeral Home

GIPSON FURNITURE CO.

I:1 1872 Wm. Gipson started in business as a cabinet maker and coffin manufacturer in the same block as the Masonic building. Each coffin was made of solid walnut and according to measurements.

He afterward was associated with A. B. Buren and in 1887 bought in as partner with Benson and Maxwell where Mattingly Bros. store is now. He bought out his partners in 1891 and the business continued to occupy the same building until 1940.

Mr. Gipson gave up active participation in the business in 1912 and his son Chas. D. Gipson has had active management since that time. At the death of Mr. Gipson the business was incorporated. In 1950 Chas. D. Gipson bought out the remaining heirs and entered in partnership with his son Chas. W. Gipson. In 1940 the business was moved from the Wettstein building where it had been for 56 years and in 1954 the Gipsons purchased the Lilly building and the business was moved to the location formerly occupied by Witten Hardware Co.

GIPSON FUNERAL HOME

The First Christian Church of Trenton

THE OLD

THE NEW

Sunday, November 15, 1953, was a momentous occasion for the First Christian Church of Trenton. One hundred years ago on that day, a small band of sincere, earnest Christians met and organized this Church which stands today as a monument to their faith and memory, and a power for good not only in our local community, but throughout our country and the world as well.

In 1847, six years previous to 1853, a small group of twenty-six people in this county founded the first organization known as the Christian Church. They continued to meet for a few years, but because of a very unhappy experience with a "bad preacher" the small group felt disgraced and disbanded the organization.

In the fall of 1853, the Rev. T. P. Haley, one of the state evangelists assigned to serve Northwest Missouri, came to Trenton where he found no Church, but found a few members of the former organization. On the third Sunday in November, 1853, about forty people organized the First Christian Church of Trenton. The Charter members were William Collier, Sr., Mrs. William Collier, Sr., Joseph Collier, William Collier, Jr., Robert Collier, Charles Collier, Mrs. Susan Collier Austin, J.H.Shanklin, Mrs. Kittie Collier Shanklin, Adam Murray, Mrs. Adam Murray, Thomas Proctor, Mrs. Thomas Proctor, M.A. Thaxton, Mrs. M.A.Thaxton, Barton England, Mrs. Barton England, Mr. Thomas, Martha Collier, Miss Sarah Templeman, Ann Cooper, Mrs. Sallie Reynolds Schooling, George Moberly, Mrs. George Moberly and D. T. Wright. (The above list includes only available names.)

The organization has had three places of worship during the century. The first, a brick building was located in the middle of the first block east of the Court House on the north side of East 7th. The deed to the property was made March 9, 1858, by George Hubbell and wife to James Terrill, John H.Shanklin and Martin Peterson, elders at that time. The cost of this building was $2,000; interest paid on loans 10%. There are many interesting stories told of the trying times in this Church.

One that is of most interest to us today is the argument for and against the use of musical instruments in the Church. All songs were led by the use of tuning fork.

The congregation worshipped in this Church for almost thirty years. They outgrew it and began looking for a new location. On May 19, 1887, Milton Crow and wife deeded to the elders of the Church two lots on the N.E. corner of what is now the corner of East Crowder Road and Mabel Street. Gilbert D. Smith, Luther Collier, and Paris 'Stepp were the elders at that time. The consideration of this transaction was one dollar, the land being an outright gift to the Church. No data is available on this Church. It was a brick building.

In 1903, the congregation decided a still larger and more modem building was needed, the present site was selected. The present building was completed and dedicated in 1903. The Rev. C. F. Stevens, who was present for the centennial program on November 15, 1953, was the pastor at that time. Several remodeling programs have been planned and executed since its dedication.

Former ministers of the Church were D.T. Wright, B. H. Smith, D. M.Tumey, H. D. Williams, Rev. Mitchell, E. V. Rice, Elder Stewart, Benjamin Lockhart, H. W. Dale, J. R. Gaff, Martin Peterson, W. H. Blanks, W. F. Barker, Elder Cornell, R. M. Messick, J. P. Davis, Thomas Henson, Granville Snell, C. F. Stevens*, S. J. White, W.A. Shullenberger*, S. G. Fisher, R. H. Helser, George Roberts, J. E. Todd*, (*living.) Herbert P. Davis, the present pastor of the Church, had the unique experience of serving the last year of the century. Under his efficient leadership, we have adopted and are following a functional plan of organization and have a new constitution; a long range building program is underway and new property has been purchased on Seventeenth Street.

Dr. Todd has the longest record of service to the Church, having served thirty-three years, retiring in the ninety-ninth year of our history.

CONNELL HARDWARE CO.

Established In 1901

The Connell Hardware Company has been North Missouri's "Headquarters for Hardware" since 1901 when 0. E. Connell established the first Connell Hardware at Trimble, Missouri.

Mr. Connell's three sons now own and operate individually owned hardwares in Trenton, Cameron, and Gower, Missouri. J. D. Connell established a Connell Hardware Co. store in Jamesport, Missouri in 1928. The Jamesport store was moved to it's present location in Trenton in 1944. 1957 finds the fourth generation of Connell's now engaged in the hardware business; a business that has served the North Missouri area as "Headquarters for Hardware" for the last 56 years.

CONNELL HARDWARE CO.

Headquarters For Hardware

THE OLD

THE NEW

Hodge Presbyterian Church

TRENTON, MISSOURI

Within the last ninety years there have been three organizations in Trenton k nown as the Presbyterian Church. The first was formed in 1851, but little is known of it except the invitation to the townspeople in the paper dated November 8, 1851, stating:

The First Presbyterian Church of Trenton, recently organized, desires to inform those in the vicinity who may wish to unite with them, that there will be an opportunity on the first Sabbath in January, next. "

In the summer of 1875, the second organization was perfected, it too, being known as the First Presbyterian Church. The meeting was held at the residence of Mr. William Donaldson, under the direction of Reverend Kennedy of Hamilton, Mo., and the following persons became members: Mr. and Mrs. William Donaldson, Mrs. Randolph, Mrs. S. Smith, and Mr. John Reid. When the membership grew to forty, they rented the old building of the M. E. Church South, and the Reverend Chandienne of Cameron was called. He served a year and was succeeded by the Reverend J. M. Crawford. In the meantime, a new church building was erected, and on Sunday, December 19, 1879, on the morning it was to be dedicated, the edifice burned to the ground, involving a loss of $6,800 to the members. The next building was erected on the corner of Elm and Prospect Streets, north of the present library.

On May 19, 1880, the present organization was formed. It was called "The Hodge Presbyterian Church. " The charter members were Mr. and Mrs. Wm. Donaldson, Mr. and Mrs. I. M. White, Mr. and Mrs. W. D. Dobson, Mr. and Mrs. John Flannigan, Mr. and Mrs. Charles Zensen, Miss Jennie Lafferty, Miss Helen Babcock, Miss Tillie McGuire, Miss Flora Tinsman, Mrs. Geo. F. Walker, Mrs. Ed Beson, Mrs. S. Smith, and Mrs. Randolph. The new organization purchased the old South Methodist Church building and had it refitted throughout at an expense of $2, 500. A church building on Chestnut Street was built in 1903 after the building they had been meeting in was blown down in a windstorm. During the period of erection, which started in November of that year, they met in the Episcopal Church.

The brick church located on Chestnut Street burned the afternoon of March 5, 1941. Due to the shortage of materials caused by World War II work on the new church was not begun until 1945. The members of the building committee were: M. E. Morris, C. C. Ebbe, Murk L. Mahaffie, W. W. Finch, T. A. Simons, Ed Walton, and H. F. Hoffman. A great debt is owed to these men for their efforts and success. The first service was held in the basement of the new church on February 8, 1948. The Reverend James A. McNeilly was called to be pastor February 18, 1948. Since then Austin Heuver and Donald Everhart have served as pastirs. The present pastor, William H. Bender was called December 4, 195 6 to take effect January 1, 1957

In May 1955 the lot east of the church was purchased for the future use and development of the church. The present manse was purchased December 1956.

Special mention should be made of the long and loyal service of Miss Daisy B. Wettstein as Sunday School secretary for 45 years who passed away March 30, 1957; Mr. Clyde C. Evans, an elder for over 40 years and also Sunday School superintendent and treasurer for many of those years; and Mr. Ben Gallup and Mr. Earl Whitnell who have been elders for 20 years and have served the church in many other capacities. The present board of elders are: Mr. Clyde C. Evans, Mr. Ed Walton, Mr. Everett Frey, Mr. Frank Hoffman, Mr. J. H. Cordes, Mr. James Walker, Mr. John Stephenson, Mr. Charles Hoffman, and Mr. John Kernahan. Other church officers are: President of the Board of Trustees-Mr. Joseph Boehner; Sunday School Superintendent-Mr. Charles Hoffman; President of the Women's Association-Mrs. James Walker; Church Treasurer and Financial Secretary-Mr. Clyde C. Evans; Moderator of Westminster Fellowship-Miss Linda Hoffman. The choir director-Mr. Donald Slater, and organist-Miss Marilyn Kidd.

LEFT to RIGHT: Jess Gonzales, Manager; Mrs. Beulah Bosley, Mrs. Lois Brantley, Miss Leola Harris, Mrs. Lorraine Peoples, Clerks; Melvin Babb, Asst. Manager; Not in Picture, Chester Johnson, Pharmacist; Christine Driskill, Gene Ism,iel, Clerks.

History of the MART CUT RATE DRUG

In 1909 Mr. E. G. Kathan purchased the drug stock from a Dr. Foster, who had been operating a drug store for many years, and opened the Kathan Drug. The building owned by Sally Patton, was purchased by Mr. and Mrs. Kathan in 1909 and a complete new front constructed in 1911.

Mr. Kathan operated the drug store until 1937, at which time he sold the store to a Mr. Scanlon of St. Joseph, Missouri. On Thanksgiving Day, 1939, Mr. Kathan took possession of the drug store again and operated it until his death in 1943.

Mrs. Kathan sold the drug store to Mr. Jim Lambert, Chillicothe, Missouri, owner of a chain of drug stores, in the spring of 1943 and he opened the MART CUT RATE DRUG.

March 1956, was the beginning of extensive remodeling and redecorating, converting the drug store into a modern up-to-date drug with a new front, new fixtures, and a new pharmacy. The formal opening was held May 5, 6, and 7, 1956, permitting thousands of customers to admire the new MART CUT RATE DRUG.

"It's Smart to Shop at Marts"

MARTS DRUGS

No. 1 Chillicothe-Tel. 167
No. 3 Kirksville-Tel. 5-3044
No. 2 Trenton-Tel. 54
No. 4 Brookfield-Tel. 22

OLD　　　　　BEFORE REMODELING　　　　　NEW

History of First Methodist Church

The First Methodist Church was organized March, 1865, by Rev. B.F. Mesner, at the home of Mr. end Mrs. S. D. Luke. Charter members included Mr. and Mrs. S. D. Luke, Mr. and Mrs. Geo. Schlotterback, Mr. and Mrs. Giles Songer, Mr. and Mrs. Wm. Songer, Mr. and Mrs. Peter Colley, Mr. and Mrs. J.F. Price and Mrs. Arabella Gibeaut. Descendants of these charter members who are now members of the present church are Mrs. Josie Breithenbutcher, granddaughter of Mr. and Mrs. S. D. Luke, Mrs. Clara Haynes, Mrs. Lulu Barry and Mrs. Nellie M. Robinson, granddaughters of Mr. and Mrs. Giles Songer. Mrs. Robinson is secretary of the present church, and prepared this statement.

Services were first held in the Baptist Church on South Main Street, then in the old court house and later in the Christian Church on what is now 7th Street, east of the court house. In 1896 a frame building costing about $2,500 was erected at the place now known as "Five Points." The lot was contributed by S.D. Luke. Three years later, 1872, the church was moved to the sight of the present building. It was enlarged and improved, and continued to be used until 1893 when, under the pastorate of Rev. J. W. Cox, the present building was erected at the cost of about $26,000. The day of the dedication the sermon was preached by Rev. Earl Cranston (afterward Bishop Cranston) of Cincinnati, Ohio. His subject was "The Majesty of God in the Church."

In 1915 under the pastorate of E.J. Gale, the 50th anniversary was observed. The services lasted from Sunday until Thursday. Judge Geo. Hall gave a full history of the church, and two former pastors were present, Rev. J.W. Goughlin, 1873-74 and Ben F. Jones, '1905-07. One charter member, Mrs. Arabella Gibeaut, was present.

In 1868, under the pastorate of Rev. Edwin Rosell, the Methodist Sunday School was organized in the old court house. N. M. Ridgeway was named superintendent, W. H. Flesher assistant, Geo. Slotterback secretary. In the years that followed R.E. Boyce was artist for the Sunday School for 40 years. G.W. McFarland librarian 53 years, missing only 7 Sundays in all that time, Homer Hall superintendent 14 years, and Miss Mary Dellman secretary for more than 20 years. During the pastorate of E.J. Gale, class 17-12 of young men and women, was organized, and responsible for the excavating of the front part of the basement and the kitchen. Superintendent of the Public School, C.A. Green and Miss Elizabeth Brainard were co-teachers. Under the pastorate of H. R. Runion the rear part of the basement was excavated and fitted up as a dining room and a Sunday School room for the junior department. Another large class was a Union class of men of several churches of Trenton which met is the court house with A. M. Hyde as teacher. Many of our most faithful laymen came to the church from this class.

In the year 1949 a bequest from the estate of Miss Dorothy Lewis was left to the church to start a fund for an educational unit. During the pastorate of A.C. Runge, contributions from the members of the church brought about the building of a room 35" by 40" oa the vacant lot north of the sanctuary, which houses the kindergarten and primary departments of the church school. This was completed and ready for use in the fall of 1953.

For Experienced Abstract And Title Insurance Work of All Kinds

R. Leroy Miller,
Owner

Elizabeth Linker,
Manager

Ruth   Saipley
Lela Elledge

TRENTON ABSTRACT COMPANY

705 MAIN

Directly Across The Street From Courthouse
On The Ground Floor

Telephone No.   17

First Baptist Church

THE OLD

THE NEW

Under the newly leafed-out branches of an elm tree standing on the south bank of Grand River, not far from what is now the foot of Main Street, a band of deeply religious pioneers gathered in May, 1838. All were newcomers to a new land, for only five years before had the first white settlers come Into the territory that was to become Grundy County.

But with them these early pioneers in the rich Grand River valley brought not only courage and fortitude but a trust in God. When their homes were built, it was only natural that they should think at once of forming an active church through which to express their religious natures.

So it was that in 1838, this group gathered to consider formation of a church. And it was there, more than a century ago, that the Baptist Church of today in Trenton was organized. This also appears to have been Trenton's very first church.

There probably were more present at this meeting than the ten who formally organized the church. Those ten were Elder Elijah Merrill, the first pastor; Nancy Merrill, James J. Merrill, Elizabeth Merrill, Samuel Benson, Matilda Benson, Cornelius Darnaby and his wife, and Jacob Oxford and his wife. Descendants of these pioneers are listed today among members of the Baptist Church of Trenton.

Early records of the church have been lost, but it has come down to the present time that the first court of Grundy County was held in an old log building near the old city cemetery, that was listed in the court records as the Baptist Church. That was in 1841.

Soon afterward, D. T. Wright built a room near where the county jail now stands, which he rented to the Baptists for their services. It was in 1850 that the church erected its own house of worship. That was on the lot at 419 South Main Street.

A BRIEF HISTORY OF THE CHURCH

This first building owned by the church was 40 feet long and 26 feet wide. It soon was insufficient for the church's needs and it was enlarged by ten feet. It was in this building that a long remembered revival was held at which 100 persons were added to the church. People who are members of the church today can recall attending services in this old building.

Originally known as the Washington United Baptist Church, the name was changed in 1875 when the church was incorporated as the First Baptist Church of Trenton. The same year a start was made for the erection of a new and larger church building. The present lot was purchased and in 1876 a Gothic type building was dedicated. The lot cost $650.00 and the church itself was put up for $5,600.00.

This building served the congregation until the arrival of the new century. In 1906 it was torn down to make way for the present structure which was dedicated in July, 1912. The new church cost about $25,000.00. and was remodeled some 38 years ago at a cost of $10,000.00.

In 1938 the church felt again the need for more room. The result was the construction of the Sunday School addition at a cost of $6,000.00. This structure, matching carefully the architecture and appearance of the main building, was dedicated during Centennial Week, May 22-29, 1938.

Pastors who have served during the 118 years of service have been Elijah Merrill, Henry M. Anderson, A. F. Martin, Terry Bradley, George W. Warmoth, P. McCollum (two times), H. H. Turner, A. Jones, J.R. Shanafelt, Robert Livingston, J.L. Cole, J. R. M. Beeson, R.L. Jamison, F.J. Leavitt, J.T. Williams, L.T. Fisher, N.B.H. Gardner, S.P. Brite, W.M. Jones, W.H. Owen, J.E. Petty, T.M.E. Kenny, J.C. Maple, T. R. Corr, J. B. Benton, C. B. Miller, Charles E. Henry, E.L. Rogers, W. H. Brengle, George L. Hale, J.C. Greenoe, William D. Hurst, Wilson Hammon, Francis Kelly and Wayne Rosecrans.

1ST ROW: Left to Right: John Thomas, Martha Barrows, Francis Hughes, Marguerite Gay, Minnie Allardice. 2ND ROW: Charles Marquis, Karen Dixon, Rex Barnett, Dorothea Lutz, Don Lewis, Clarence "Wamp" William.

THE FAIR DRUG STORE

1906 ---1957

This Drug Store at this location has served the people in Trenton and around Trenton for the betterment of their health for a Half-Century. We hope to give the people as good, if not better service the next Half-Century. We now have one of the largest Prescription Departments in the northwest part of the state, and a Registered Pharmacist on duty at all times for the protection, and betterment of your health.

Our store has been known as FAIR DRUG STORE for many years, and now as THE FAIR DRUG STORE. Now owned and operated by - Mr. & Mrs. L. C. Carpenter and Mr. & Mrs. Charles Marquis for the past two years.

Immanuel Lutheran Church

Trenton, Missouri

Immanuel Lutheran Church, a member congregation of The Lutheran Church - Missouri Synod, was organized in 1950. Charter members of the congregation were: Elmer Fick, Trenton; Clarence Meinke, Princeton; Elvin Moll, Trenton; Adolph Moll, Trenton; Theodore Ahrends, Spickard; Howard Lietz, Trenton; Gerald Meinke, Princeton; Louis Meinke, Sr., Princeton; Kenneth Meinke, Princeton; Elmer Meinke, Princeton; Conrad Rynell, Trenton.

Since its organization, the congregation has been served from Chillicothe by the Rev. Walter J. Lotz, pastor of St. John's Lutheran Church of that city.

The first minister of the group was the Rev. Fred. C. Stein, who has been a chaplain with the United States Air Force since 1944 and is now serving a unit in French Morocco. He was succeeded by the Rev. Walter F. Strickert, who, since 1949, is serving St. Paul's Lutheran Church of Sedalia.

The congregation has no church of its own. It has conducted its services at the V. F. W. Hall, in the basement of the old Presbyterian Church, and at the American Legion Hall. At present the congregation worships at the Trenton Methodist Church on the 2nd and 4th Sundays of the month at 7:30 p. m. A building fund owned by the congregation has been temporarily invested in the Church Extension Fund of the Missouri Synod.

The church, which numbers 23 members, is served by the following officers; Elmer Fick, Pres. ; Gerald Meinke, Sec. ; Kenneth Meinke, Treas.; Elmer Meinke, Fin. Sec.; Carl Guenther, Louis Meinke, Kenneth Meinke, Elders.

Goffe & Carkener, Inc.
Established 1893
Investments - Stocks - Bonds - Mutual
Funds - Commodity Futures - Wholesale
Cash Grains - Minimum Commissions
"Personalized Service"
Glenda F. Keith - E. E. Kauffman - Patsy Hatfield

Left to Right: Willard Bosley, Charles Rosson, Joe Cummings, Ralph Newgent.

For The Best in Dairy Products

Grade "A" Pasteurized, Homogenized Milk
St erilized Whipping Cream
Fortified "Non-Fat" Skim Milk

Half & Half
Chocolate Milk
Cottage Cheese

Coffee Cream
Buttermilk
Butter

American Cheese Slices
Cheddar Squares

Tropicana Orange Juice
Sunkist Lemonade

Delicious Ice Cream (Smooth Freeze)
LOOK FOR

Meadow Gold

At Your Grocers
By

BEATRICE FOODS CO.

Phone 228

History of the Church of the Nazarene

In 1927 a group of people were meeting in a humble little building in the 700 block on Highland Avenue. They were not affiliated with any denomination at that time and no one was officially serving as pastor.

Through the official paper of the Church of the Nazarene called "Herald of Holiness", Reverend P. P. Belew of Gary, Indiana was called to hold a ten day revival. After the revival they were directed to call Reverend P. C. Norton of Gilman to come and pastor the mission. He came every Saturday even though it required that he walk the last five miles, because of poor transportation facilities.

It was August 16, 1929 at the home of Mr. and Mrs. Vernal Ralston that the mission was officially organized into the Church of the Nazarene. It was organized with twelve charter members. They were Mr. and Mrs. Vernal Ralston, Mrs. Lon Clemens, Mrs. H. D. Shively, Mrs. Fannie Chandle, Mrs. Cynthis Klingensmith, Mrs. Della Whitworth, Mr. William Klingensmith, Mrs. Bessie Gannon, Ruby Chandler, and Mrs. Laura Mack.

There have been ten pastors of the church since its official organization. They are Reverends P. C. Norton, E. L. Askins, L. A. Windsor, John Warner, C. B. Wison, V. C. Ralston, Fred Easley, Earl A. Vansickle, Parker Craig and Hugh Bright the present pastor.

There have been three places of worship since their beginning. First was in the 700 block on Highland Avenue; the stone church at 15th and Carnes was purchased and used until their present building at 22nd & Chicago was built. The present church building was dedicated in August of 1955.

Moore & Clark Insurance Agency

908 Main St.   Phone 136

The Moore and Clark Insurance Agency was established in 1937 by the late W. P. (Bill) Moore.. In May of 1952, Bill Moore passed away, and on January 1, 1953, Bill J. Clark Joined Mrs. Moore to form a partnership. This Agency sells all kinds of insurance, including Fire, Casualty, Accident and Health and Hospitalization, and Life insurance. Pictured above, left to right, are Mrs. Rita Hobbs, Mrs. Moore, and Mr. Clark.

STANDING: J. F. Nickels, Bonnie Shaw, Lois Crawford, Dena Mae Allison, Martha Norris, Edith Ricketts, Lois Murray, Arline Long, Ruby Fitzpatrick, Wanda Dillinger, Dorothy Webster, Emma Kelly, Lucille Reeves, Letha Chumley, Daphne Hartley, Oma Harrin, Edith Kelly, Marie Ralston, Laura Mae Terhune, Elizabeth Nickels, Bettie Cahill. KNEELING: Ernie Peoples, Forrest Kinnison, Dale Dennis, Sam Kemp, Joe Hamilton, Vernon McCollum. (Not Present - Bob Winter)

Mr. Jim Cahill came to Trenton in July 1925. From the date of his arrival until 1927 he was employed by the Trenton Gas & Electric Co.

In March of 1927 he bought the laundry, located on Tinsman Avenue, from John Rose, at that time there were 6 employees. Within a year the machinery had been changed and the staff was increased to 10.

In April of 1932, the plant was moved to the Flesher building on East 12th St.

The company moved to the present location in 1939 and purchased the building from the Trenton National Bank. The building was constructed of brick from the Brick Kiln that at one time operated in Trenton. It had previously been occupied by a grocery store and a tire shop. The corner office was a 2 story building and the second floor, at one time, housed the colored Masons. The second floor was removed and the materials used to build on to the east side. In 1946, a house on the east was purchased, dismantled and another addition was made to bring the plant to its present size.

Service Laundry & Cleaners

Member of American Institute of Laundering
Member of National Institute of Dry Cleaners

History of the United Brethren Church

In November of 1944, the pastor and congregation began a new journey. This new journey started by the purchasing of a building site for a new church during the month of November, 1944.

This site covers one-half block and is paved on three sides. There was a massive house standing on the site. The cost of this property was $4500.00. The work of dismantling the house was done by members and friends of the church. All materials from the old house were salvaged and much of it used in construction of the new building. The first brick in the church was put in place on May 3, 1946. The building was completed and dedicated in March of 1947.

The building, including the building site, cost the sum of $39, 695.59. At present values it is conservatively estimated that the property is worth $75, 000. 00. The church has a modern six room apartment on the second floor of the educational unit. This Is used as a home for the pastor and family.

During the past years Sunday School attendance has tripled. The church roll has been completely revised and in recent years more than 100 new names hve beena added to the roll

Present membership is 170. This total includes the non-resident members.

The history of the United Brethren Church in Trenton dates back to the late 1800's. In 1890, there were two progressive United Brethren Churches in Trenton, one of them on the north side of town called the Holt Church, the other on the east side in connection with Avalon College.

The denomination decided in 1890 to move the college to Trenton from Avalon. The college was built on the site of the present Trenton Junior College and high school buildings. The College Avenue Church is now owned by the Latter Day Saint's group but is still in good condition and the original cornerstone, indicating the forma ownership by the United Brethren Church, is still in the building.

The college was closed in 1900 but the two churches continued to function. About 1918 it was thought best to merge the two churches and build one nearer the center of town. The new church building on the corner of Ninth and Halliburton Streets was dedicated in 1921 with the Reverend T. M. Johnson as pastor. The congregation worshiped in this building until 1942 when this building was sold for a site to the Co-Op Oil Company, and a piece of property was purchased at 314 W. Crowder Road.

This was a large house and was used both as a chapel and pastor's residence until the spring of 1946, when this building.was sold and the congregation met in the V. F. W. Hall until they were able to meet in their new building on Ninth and McPherson Streets. In September, 1944, Dr. C. H. Crandall, who was also Conference Superintendent, came to Trenton as the pastor .

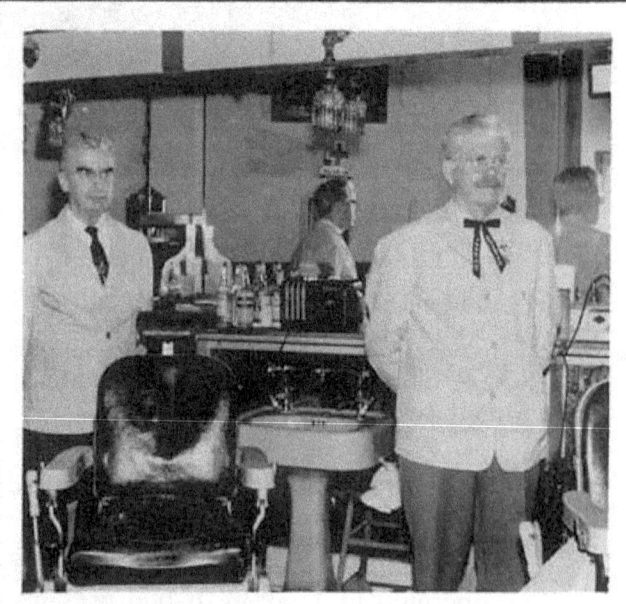

At Five Points 27 Years

Bonta & Noel Barber Shop

F. W. Bonta   O. T. Noel

LEFT TO RIGHT: L. D. Menefee D. D. S. , Forrest C. Cox D. D. S. , Ted E. Ritze D.D.S. and Sam S. Tolle D. D. S. Insert Maurice B. Embry D.D.S. now in service with the U. S. Air Force and will return to Trenton this summer.

CENTENNIAL GREETINGS

The Dentists of Trenton

Early Dentists in Trenton

Prior to the visiting of Dr. A. C. Green, traveling dentist, teeth were generally treated and extracted by M.D. 's . Dr. Green usually stopped at the Proctor House and set up office for a few days each month. He was the first dentist registered in' Trenton. He was followed by Drs. Steckman, Shotwell, Boatman and Robinson who were permanently located in the community. In 1901 Dr. Wannamaker came to Trenton, followed by Dr. Hemley in 1902. In 1909 Dr. Merryman and Dr. Wettstein opened offices in the Kress Building. In the early 1900's during the World War period, Drs. Taylor, Adams, Orr, Duncan, Nair and Anderson were located briefly in Trenton. Dr. Clark opened his office in 1923 followed by Dr. Cox in 19 24 . Dr, Menefee opened in 1926 and Dr. Tolle in 1930, followed by Dr. Embry in 1938. Dr. Ritze opened his office in 1946. Dr. McCue practised from 1929 until 1930 and Dr. Hasting was in Trenton for four years from 1940 until 1943. Dr. Davis also practised from 1953 until 1955.

History of St. Joseph Catholic Church

THE OLD

THE NEW

The Catholic families here in the early days were never great in number, perhaps thirty to thirty-five families. The first settlers were Irish or Irish descent, and in order to verify this fact one has only to go to the Catholic cemetery and look at the names on the tombstones.

According to the records which we have on hand, the Catholic Church here was erected in the year 1872, and at that time in a frame building. It was dedicated by Bishop Hogan in 1874. In 1918 the church was renovated and replaced by a brick veneer which is the present structure of the building.

Many priests served this parish down through the years. The first pastor was Rev. J. J. Kennedy. He served from 1872 to 1882; Rev. James Mulvey from 1882 to 1889; Rev. W. M. McCormack from 1889 to 1896; Rev. J. J. Burke from 1896 to 1889; Rev. J. D. O'Donnell from 1889 to 1902; Rev. T. Ahearn from 1902 to 1906; Rev. Henry B. Tierney, from 1906 to 1926; The Reverend Patrick O'Shea, from 1926 to 1932; The Reverend Martin Vonderstein, from 1932 to 1935; Rev. Cornelius A. Curry, from 1935 to 1939; The Reverend John r. Kenny from 1939 to 19 42 . The present pastor, Father John P. Gallagher, was appointed to this parish July 18, 1942.

The Saint Joseph's Parish is now composed of seven different nationalities, and its membership has tripled during the past eight years.

Flesher
Sheet Metal Works

Since 1920
I Fabricate My Own Duct Work In My
Shop So Your job Is Custom Made,
Air Conditioning In Connection With
Heating System If You Wish
1300 Lulu - Tel. 687

Centennial Greetings

CAFETERIA

VIEW FROM SOUTH

OFFICE

PLANT FROM WEST PARKING AREA

TRENTON FOODS, INC.

St. Philip's Episcopal Church

The present church building was built in 18,J8 during the pastorate of the Rev. Henry Duboc but the church organization was begun several years prior to that time with services held in the Masonic Hall. The church building is made of native stone and in 1928 on its 30th anniversary, a beautiful stone cross was erected on the roof. Bishop Sidney Partridge was in charge of the dedication ceremony for the cross.

The Rev. H. A. Duboc took up his permanent residence in Trenton in 189S and on April 1, 1897 he began to hold weekly Sunday services in the church. The Rev. Mr. Duboc resigned in 1900 and was succeeded by the Rev. A. B. Perry. He was succeeded by the Rev. E. U. Brun who was pastor until 1906.

A record in the parish register of the church shows the following Trenton people on an early committee in charge of the church: Warden; H. C. Kentner; Treasurer; Dr. Thomas Kimlin; Secretary; George T. McGrath, and committed members; Dr. Earl Conner and M. Sherwood.

Archdeacon Albert Watkins was in charge of the church from 1923 to 1929 and again from 1931 to 1934, when the Rev. W. M. Hargis took up the work in the district, holding services once a month at St. Philip's, with his headquarters in Chillicothe. He served until January 1, 1942.

Several ministers had charge of the church through the following years and on November 12th, 1950, the Rev. R. B. Gribbon became Vicar by the appointment of Bishop E. R. WeUes of Kansas City.

The Rev. Stuart C. Cowles succeeded Mr. Gribbon on November 1, 1954, and is the present minister in charge of the parish. Mr. Cowles is resident in Chillicothe but weekly Sunday services are held by him at St. Philip's Church. These services are alternately in the morning and afternoon each week.

Dr. Edgar A. Duffy is the present Warden of the church, Mr. Nelle Hafford is the Secretary, and Mr. John Caldwell is the Treasurer.

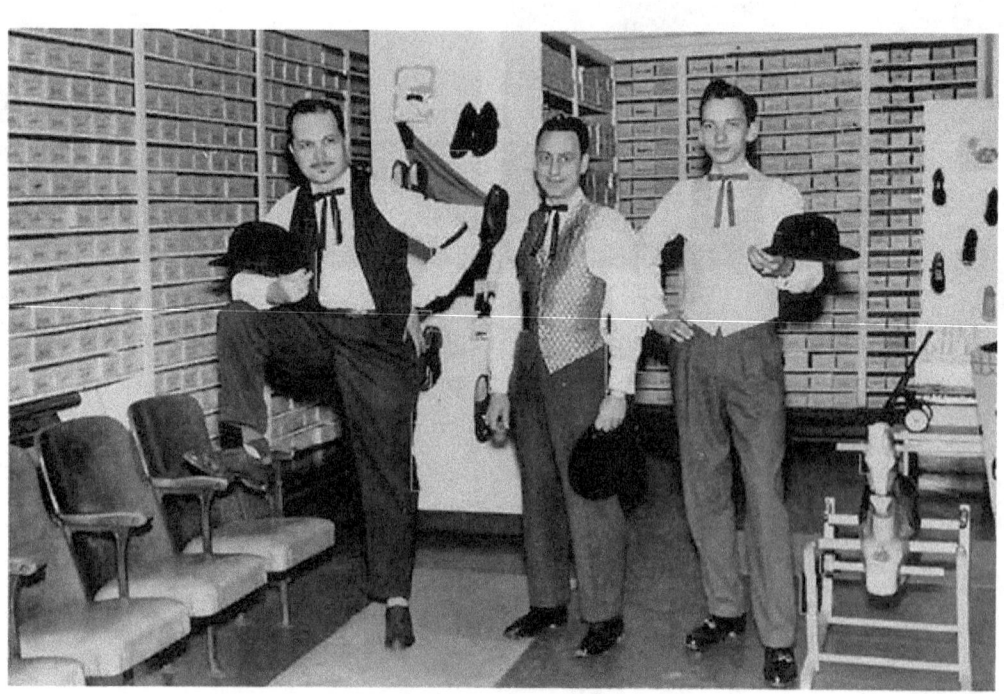

H & E Shoes
FOR ALL THE FAMILY - TRENTON'S OLDEST

CENTENNIAL GREETINGS

From The M. D.'s of Trenton

BACK ROW: Left to Right; Oliver F. Duffy M. D., E. J. Mairs M.D., David M. Witten M. D. FRONT ROW: E. A. Duffy M. D., William A. Fuson M. D., C. L. Clark M. D., C. H. Cullers M. D., H. C. Kimberlin, M. D.

History of The Assembly of God Church

The Assembly of God Church, formerly called the Pentecostal Church, originated approximately forty years ago. It was then located on Highland Ave. There were around eight or ten charter members. Among those were Mrs. Amos Fisher, Mrs. Ivy Eckerson, Mrs. Elsie Kelly, Mrs. Hannah Keith, Mrs. Lillian Brunt, a Mrs. Wilson, Mr. & Mrs. Thompson Walker, Mr. & Mrs. Sam Avery. and Mr. Chriss Keith. The church remained at this location approximately seven or eight years. During that time a large tent was stretched on 17th Street and Miss Katie Utiger, now Mrs. Glen McClure, was the evangelist. From this meeting several more members were added. A new building was constructed on Laclede Street In 1925.

The Church was set in order July 12, 1926 with a membership of 50, and affiliated with the General Council of the Assemblies of God with headquarters at Springfield, Missouri, and became known then as the Assembly of God. At this time the Rev. A. F. Crouch was called as pastor. The church remained at this location until a new lot was purchased on March 24, 1939 and a new building constructed at 1310 Main Street, and church and parsonage were moved into in the fall of '41. The pastors then were Rev. & Mrs. Glen McClure. There are now 162 active and honorary members with an average Sunday School attendance of 200. The deacons are Orville Gannon, C. C. Walker, Charlie Miller, Pearl Smith and Leland Hill. The present Pastor is Rev. Norman F. Brewer.

LEFT TO RIGHT: Dorthy Lewis, Betty Graham, Alta Irvin, Lillie Stevens.

For The future As Well As In The Centennial Year
Dinners - Short Orders - Soft Drinks
Home Cooked Meals Are Our Specialty - Dorothy Lewis, Owner

Victory Cafe

PERSONNEL

FRONT ROW: Johnny Sheets, Robert Sheets.   2ND ROW: Helen Bass, Pat Patterson, Jaunita Lewis.   3RD ROW: Ruby Nigh, Gladys Trump, Hazel King, Coral Shockey.   4TH ROW: Mgr. John A. Sheets, Sylvia Karr, Maxine Mosier, Myrtle Foster, Evelyn Sheets, Grace Brown, Lois Loutzenhi ser , Assistant Mgr. John Gardner.

MATTINGLY'S

Mattingly Brothers Stores Company is the result of the enterprise and initiative of a family of five brothers. The Company was opened with a one store unit in Odessa, Mo. , on April 4, 1914, by Mr. and Mrs. Roy Mattingly and Mr. Harry Mattingly. When this first unit, known as The Broken Dollar Store", was founded, local merchants there were skeptical and predicted the newcomers would stay in business thirty days. The reason for this dim view was that in Odessa at that time, a cash store was a very new and daring thing, People were in the habit of charging everything. Hence, the glum prophecy that the Broken Dollar Store would break the Mattinglys.

Encouraged by the success of the Odessa venture , the firm opened a second store in Glasgow, Mo. , a year later, in Feb. of 191 5 , with Mr. Hugh Mattingly in charge. Mr. Ernest Mattingly joined the organization as Manager of the Glasgow store when Mr. Hugh entered the service during World War I. Other stores were opened as quickly as good sites became available. This chain of stores was expanded as a partnership organization until the year 1927, when the tenth store was purchased, and was then incorporated and became known as Mattingly Brothers Stores Company, Incorporated.

From the one store founded in 1914 until the present time, this organization has parlayed the original investment of $1,400 into a chain ownership of 35 Variety stores and one junior Department Store, now making them the largest regional variety chain in Missouri. In May of 1957, another store will open in Marshall, Missouri. Mr. Hugh Mattingly, President, states that his firm plans further growth and would as soon open 35 more stores when and if the right locations are found.

The Trenton, Mo. , store opened as Unit #20 in 1937. Mr. John W. Sheets, the present Manager, has been located in Trenton since 1948.

First Church of Christ Scientist

The first date of interest in Christian Science appeared to be the Autumn of 1699. The circumstances connected with this instance were three loyal Christian Scientists who persistently held services in their homes. The early members were Miss Grace Callison, Miss Hattie Neeley and Mrs. William Fish. The earliest Practitioner was Miss Hattie Neeley.

The first meetings or services were in the Fall of 1899, and organization about 1911. It was called the Christian Science Society.

Charter members were Miss Grace Callison, Mrs. Ella Kull and Mrs. Blanche folly.

The first Christian Science Lecture was by Mr. Frank Leonard in January of 1913.

The Christian Science Society purchased the present property at 302 East Seventh Street in June 1938. Dedication of the Edifice was December 14, 1941. Edifice was remodeled in September 1950.

The Christian Science Society of Trenton was recognized as First Church of Christ Scientist, Trenton, Missouri, by The Mother Church of Christ Scientist, Boston, Mass, in July of 1951.

Mrs. Ella Kull is the only living Charter member of First Church of Christ Scientist, Trenton.

Mrs. Clarice Kurtz, daughter of Mrs. Blancha Jolly, Mrs. LyndaLl Miller Barnes a niece of Mrs. Jolly's, and Mrs. LyndalL Barnes daughters, Miss Carolyn Miller and Mrs. Garnet Lee Babb Hawkins are members of First Church of Christ Scientist, Trenton.

Don Crawford-Ditching Contractor

STORE PERSONNEL STANDING, Left to Right Charles R. Smith, Jr. Partner; Mrs. Margaret Topscott, Saleslady; Miss Bertha Mason, Boy Scout Manager; Mrs. Faith Babb, Hosiery Buyer; Mrs. Eva Holcomb, Bookkeeper; Mrs. Fern McClintlc, Saleslady; Clifford Hickman, Merchandise Manager. SEATED: Elmer J. Smith, Sr. Partner.

History of 53 Years of Service

Founded 53 years ago by Mr. Tom Rader and Co., this store since 1904-has served Grundy and adjacent counties, supplying men's clothing needs.

Next owners, Mr. Ed Patterson and Mr. B. C. Nichols, operated the store for 10 years before selling 1/3 interest to Mr. Elmer J. Smith in 1917, thus forming the Patterson-Nichols Co. This company operated for 11 years until the death of Mr. Patterson.

In 1928, Elmer Smith purchased the interests of Ed Patterson and B. C. Nichols and changed the firm name to E. J. Smith, Clothier. Under his management much was done to contribute to the growth of the business and the town of Trenton.

Boys' wear, work clothes, rubber footwear and athletic equipment were added to better serve the people of the community for the next 18 years.

In 1946, upon returning home from the Naval Air Corps, Charles R. Smith purchased 1/2 interest in the business. This partnership of father and son has continued up to the present time. A new Self Service Basement operation is being opened featuring *work* clothing, rubber footwear, shoes, boys' wear and Scout supplies.

DURING YOUR CENTENNIAL VISIT, WE INVITE YOU TO VISIT OUR STORE AND SEE HOW WE PLAN TO SERVE YOU BETTER IN YEARS TO COME.

SMITH'S

Men's & Boy's Clothiers

Tenth Street Baptist Church

Architects Drawing of Completed Church

This is one of Trenton's newest churches for It was as recent as 1941 that efforts on the part of several devoted people resulted in the establishment of a mission Sunday School which has grown into a full time house of worship.

At the request of Reverend W. D. Hurst, pastor of the First Baptist Church, Reverend M. F. Poland, then pastor of Zion and Rural Dale Baptist Churches, took a census and found some 350 people interested in a Sunday School. Some 15 or 20 people pledged one dollar per month for rent and miscellaneous expenses of a property at 926 Avalon.

A revival meeting in February of 1941 was conducted by Reverend and Mrs. A. H. Smith with Mr. Poland serving as song leader. This resulted in the establishment of a Sunday School the following month. On the day the Sunday School was organized 13 were present, there was an offering of 65 cents and John Allen Lewis was elected superintendent. The meeting closed with 26 converts.

The church was organized in October of 1941 as the Broyles Memorial Church and the 15 charter members follow Frank Huffstutter, Ethel Boone, Lottie Boone, Audrey Boone John Flesher, Everett Harris, Gladys Harris, Fern Harris Francis Harris,- Ervin Harris, Kate Beckner, loan Boone Mary Boone and Ruby Huffstutter. A training union was organized the same month.

In August of 1943 request for admission in the North Grand River Association was made and granted. Later the same month, the name was changed from BroylesMemorial Church to Tenth Street Baptist Church. Reverend Rex I.1. Henderson was called as pastor in January of 1944 and the following month saw the organization of a Women's Missionary Union with 11 persons attending and electing Mrs. Gladys Harris, president.

The church was incorporated in June of 1944 and the building was purchased in December of the same year for $1,000. In May of 1945 Reverend Henderson resigned as pastor to be replaced the following month by Reverend Paul M. Walters, The $650 note on the building was paid in full in May of 1947.

Reverend B. H. Walker replaced Reverend Walters as pastor in July of 1950. In February of 1951 deacons of the church recommended bonds be Issued to begin the first unit of a new church building. The old building was moved so the new one could be on the corner of Tenth and Avalon.

Board of Directors
1957
Ed Hundley . Pre s.
Willis Alexander Jr.
Ernie Arnold
Wilbur Austin
Joe Boehrier
Joe Cook, Mayor
Robert Cullers
Don Eads
Dr. Wm. A. Fuson
Helen Hall
Craig Harrison
Frank Hoffman
Carl Muff
Sam M M. Rissler
George Stone
Jerrold Stuart
I. A. Searcy, Secy.

For A Better Trenton   Get Acquainted With Your Neighbor - You Might Like Him

Trenton Chamber of Commerce
Incorporated

617 Main   Phone 8S   Trenton, Missouri

Davina Kemp - G. H. McCullough - J. A. Rider - Nelda Steele

Every Kind Of Insurance

Since 1932

Capital. Stock Companies

G. H. McCULLOUGH

INSURANCE

904 Main Street   Phone 1068

TRENTON, MISSOURI

Reorganized Church of Jesus Christ Of Latter Day Saints

Perhaps the history of this church is more closely linked with the life of Mrs. T. D. Proffit, still a resident of Trenton, than with any other person. Mrs. Proffit came to Trenton in March of 1898 with her husband who was not then a member. Soon, she wrote for a missionary to come and do some preaching" as the result of interest shown in Trenton toward this church.

Ammon White, in Cameron at that time, "began in the true old-fashioned missionary way by preaching on the streets a few times". Mrs. Proffit gave Mr. White $5.00 with which he purchased some tracts. In the process of distributing these he found Phoebe Jane Baker who was eager to help.

Probably the first actual site in Trenton was Mrs. Proffit's home on 207 Ann street, (now 313 East Eleventh), where a sign was tacked up which read, "Cottage meetings every evening ... The first tent meeting was held on the vacant lot on which presently stands the First Baptist Church in 1902. During this and numerous other meetings the church membership grew. Mrs. Proffit was the first Sunday School superintendent, taking this office in 1908.

Many missionaries and others helped the church grow continually and in August of 1909 Elder William Lewis organized the local group into a branch church at the home of Phoebe Jane Baker. This organization occurred on the present site occupied by the McVay Motor Company in the shade of an old maple tree. The 13 members present were Phoebe Jane Baker, J. W. Kelly, and wife Laura Jane and daughter Hattie Mae;. George E. Whitehead, wife Ethel and daughter Nancy 0. , and son Daniel; Bertie Baugh and daughter Beulah, and J. D. Proffit, wife Hattie B. and daughter Jaunita. At that meeting, Elder Proffit was chosen pastor of the church.

From the date of organization, meetings were held in cottages, Cutlip Hall, Miller Hall, the 1. 0. 0. F. Hall and the City Hall, until 1918 when A. S. Salyards came to Trenton and raised $1, 700 to purchase property.

(Continued On Page 36)

DONALD BARNES

HUGH BARNES

Barnes Greenhouses

Since 1904
Wholesale Vegetable and Flower Plants

Trenton and Chillicothe, Missouri

FREE DELIVERY   PHONE 175

DAVIS FOOD-CENTER

Trenton's-Lowest-Food-Prices

127 YEARS - NOT JUST 100

One hundred twenty-seven years experience and know-how. Trenton's senior home owned food store operated by Thelma and Muriel Davis began May, 1939. We are very pleased and happy to say many of our friends who became customers 18 years ago are still with us. We truly feel that each and every customer, old or new, is a personal friend, and we enjoy this friendship very much.

One hundred twenty-seven years, that is how much experience and know-how you receive at Davis.

It has always been store policy to hire the very best and most experienced help available. Each a true expert in this particular line of the food business. We are Thelma and Muriel Davis, Mr. Ed. Kunder, L. A. Whitney, Sarah and Melvin Dockery, Raymond Beery and John Eichert.

"FOLKS LIKE TO SHOP AT DAVIS AND WE LOVE TO HAVE YOU"

Thanks
Thelma and Muriel

CENTENNIAL GREETINGS FROM

BACK ROW: (Left to Right) Gerald Long, Orville Arbuckle, Russell Ellis. FRONT ROW: Eddie Knudsen, Hugh Graham, Richard Laffoon. EMPLOYEE NOT SHOWN: Orange Spears.

The feed plant and soybean mill was built in 1945, and handles Purina products.

The Ralston Purina Feed Company was founded by William H. Danforth, more than 63 years ago. Mr. Danforth's burning desire to make a balance ration for livestock, started a small feed business on the banks of the Mississippi River, with nothing more than a scoop shovel and a strong determination.

Today the Ralston Purina Feed Company is the world's largest feed manufacturing company, with approximately 50 mills in operation in the United States, Canada, Old Mexico and South America. It also has the largest laboratory and research farm of its kind.

CENTRAL FARM PRODUCTS CO.

FRONT ROW: Ralph Pettis, Henry Fischer, Donald Osborne, Rafael Stokes, Aleck Pettengill, Leroy Allison, Doyle Spencer, Robert Osborn, Vermal Brown, Ronald Tolle, Eugene Stiles. SECOND ROW: Larry Walsh, Howard Osborn, Richard Mitchell, Mack Dockery, Arthur Arneson, James Whitworth, Leland Ellis, Floyd Stottlemyre, Roy Wilford, Donald Washburn, Raymond Wilford, Edwin Knudsen, Eric Sonnich, Harlie Reid, Richard O'Halloran. THIRD ROW: Mrs. Ralph Walsh, Luther Dysart, Mrs. Leland McCully. EMPLOYEES NOT SHOWN: Victor Williams, Albert Gardner, Billy Barlow, Franklin Brown, Robert Jackson, David Mitchell, Robert Owens, Frank Kirkman.

LEADING BUYERS OF WHOLE MILK IN NORTH MISSOURI AND SOUTHERN IOWA

TRENTON PHONE 77

A view from the clock tower shows the Rock Island Shops

Established 1879. Reverend Hardin Morton pastor. There were 12 charter members, at that time. It was known as the Second Baptist Church. Later under the pastorate of Reverend A. M. Smith the name was changed to Merrill St. Baptist Church.

Some of the charter members were - Mrs. Susan Henry, Vicey Walker, Martha Henderson, Alice and Lucy Robinson. Although the present membership is only eight, the church is progressing nicely under the leadership of the Reverend Author Smith.

(Continued From Page 32)

A committee from the Latter Day Saints church and a similar committee from the United Brethren in Christ church met and negotiated a sale of the current building for $3,500. The $1,700 was paid and the balance of $1,800 was carried by deed of trust. The last dollar of the note was liquidated In October of 1939.

After a continuous leadership of seventeen and one-half years, W. Profflt resigned and J. R. Lentell of Lamoni, Iowa was chosen to replace him. Two years later, he was followed by E. E. Garnet who served until 1935. The current pastor Is Elder Alan Tyree of Columbia, Mo. Sunday services are conducted by Walter Strange of Humphreys. Present membership is 60. Mr. Proffit after 17 years went on as pastor and assistant pastor for 47 years. At the time of his passing he was assistant pastor. Alwayg end up with this creed; our creed all truth.

It Pays To Look Well

Walkers Barber Shop

Elza Walker

Dwight Walker - Sherman Cox

Keen Coal Co.

Coal - Oil   - Scrap

1945   1957

STANDIiJG: Left to Right: George Stone, Owner; C. R. Meeks, Body Shop Forman; Charles Duncan, Harlen Hobbs, Service Manager; Ronald Ishmael, Shop Forman; Robert Ballinger, C. L. Morrison. SEATED: Gracie Gibler, C. E. Desper, Office Manager.

The Stone Motor Co. was started Inthe spring of 1937 with our location in the building now occupied by the A & P Store at 9th and Washington. In 1942, not having automobiles to sell, we moved from this location to a smaller building on 10th street where repair service was continued. In 1946 a New, modern, up-to-date brick building was constructed for the Sales and Service of New and Used automobiles. We have enjoyed thirty years in Trenton as Buick and Pontiac automobiles dealer.

 # STONE MOTORS

The Howell Hanging

In all her history, Grundy county has had but one hanging, and it is safe to say that there will never be another lawful hanging within her limits. This is the only tragic event that this history will mention, for to enumerate them would fill a volume.

Joseph A. Howell was accused of the murder of Mrs. Minnie Pall and her four children, in Linn county, January 19, 1890, afterwards allegedly setting fire to their home and burning the bodies. For three years the trial dragged out, finally coming to Grundy county by change of venue. There has always been doubt in the minds of some whether Howell was guilty. But guilty or not, he was sentenced to hang August 10, 1893, and a special boarded enclosure was erected adjacent to the jail on the east part of the courthouse square.

Precisely at ten o'clock, the cell door of Joseph A. Howell was thrown open and, attended by his guards, spiritual advisers, counsel, and friends, he walked forth for the first time in many months, not as a free man but as one who was soon to be freed. He was walking to his grave.

The Reverend J. H. Cox, Reverend T. M. S. Kenney, and E. M. Harber of his counsel, walked in front, and following came the doomed man supported on either side by Sheriff Winters and A, D. Bally, U. S. Marshal, F. M. Marshall, of St. Joseph, and Sheriff J. W. White of Macon. At the head of the stairs, they were met by A. G. Knight, another of the defendant's counsel.

The doomed man was led directly to the trap, where he was supported for an instant until he recovered from the fatigue of climbing the stairs. The sun beat down unmercifully, and his head was shaded by a friend; his face was deathly pale and as he stood there in the glare of the burning sun, there were but few hearts that beat with anything but pity for him, He first turned to Mr, Bally, and shaking hands, he bade him farewell. Turning to Mr. Harber he handed him his buttonhole bouquet, together with a sealed package, and bade him goodbye. Turning to the sheriff, he said, "All that I have to say has been written by me. Goodbye." (He had written his life story which was published and sold to pay for the expense of the trial and burial.)

W. N. Winters and G. Heinan, two deputies, at once began to adjust the straps that pinioned his arms and legs during which he stood still, though wavering slightly. When this was finished, Sheriff Winters took the black cap from his pocket and as he started to place it over the head of the condemned man, the latter's lips quivered slightly and it appeared as if he was trying to utter a prayer. When the cap was adjusted, Reverend Cox stepped to his side, and with Reverend Kenney began to repeat the Lord's prayer. The front of the black cap apparently fluttered as if the doomed man was uniting in the prayer. In the meantime, Sheriff Winters stepped to the lever which held the trap in place. Never more solemn, nor full of meaning, did the words sound, "for thine is the glory forever, Amen. " The prayer was finished and the soul of Joseph Howell had been launched upon the dark journey.

The drop fell at 10:10 a.m. , and Drs. Coon and Hendrickson immediately stepped forward and began to take the pulsations. In eight minutes he was pronounced dead, and three minutes later the body was cut down by Dr. Coon. Undertaker Wm. Gipson immediately took charge of the remains, and within half an hour they were carried, enclosed in a neat casket, to a shady place in the courthouse yard, where thousands of people viewed the remains.

In accordance with the announcement made by the Reverend Cox from the scaffold, the funeral procession departed from the courthouse yard at 3:00 p.m. In the following order: Reverend J. H. Cox of the M. E. Church and T. M. S. Kenney of the Baptist Church; the hearse bearing the remains; pallbearers consisting of M. Wolz, J.F. Carter, Millard Steele, Wesley Williams, A. D. Bailey, and J. W. Schooler; carriage containing Messrs. Harber and Knight and Sheriff Winters. At least five thousand people were at the cemetery. "Never was a man who died under such circumstance given a more respectable burial . "

Early War Veterans

The Fourth of July celebration in 1870 saw the appearance of four soldiers of the War of 1812 on the platform. They were David Plumbley of Franklin township, known as "Uncle Davy"; William Collier, Sr. age 78, and a long resident of Trenton; William N. Smith, 78, an old settler of Missouri; John Estes of Kentucky, who was on a visit to his son, Capt. J. S. Estes. All of these with the exception of Estes, were in the Indian wars also.

Cold Snaps

Trenton can boast of some cold weather. The year 1889 was exceptional In this line. In February, the record temperature of 32 degrees below zero was recorded, and for a week's duration the thermometer never rose above 25 degrees below.

Overton Dist. Co.
Trenton, Missouri

Distributor

BUDWEISER-BUSCH BAVARIAN

BEERS
For Below Named Counties

GRUNDY	HARRIS ON
MERCER	LIVINGSTON
DAVIES	S ULLIVAN
CALDWELL	PUTNAM

James H. Overton, Owner

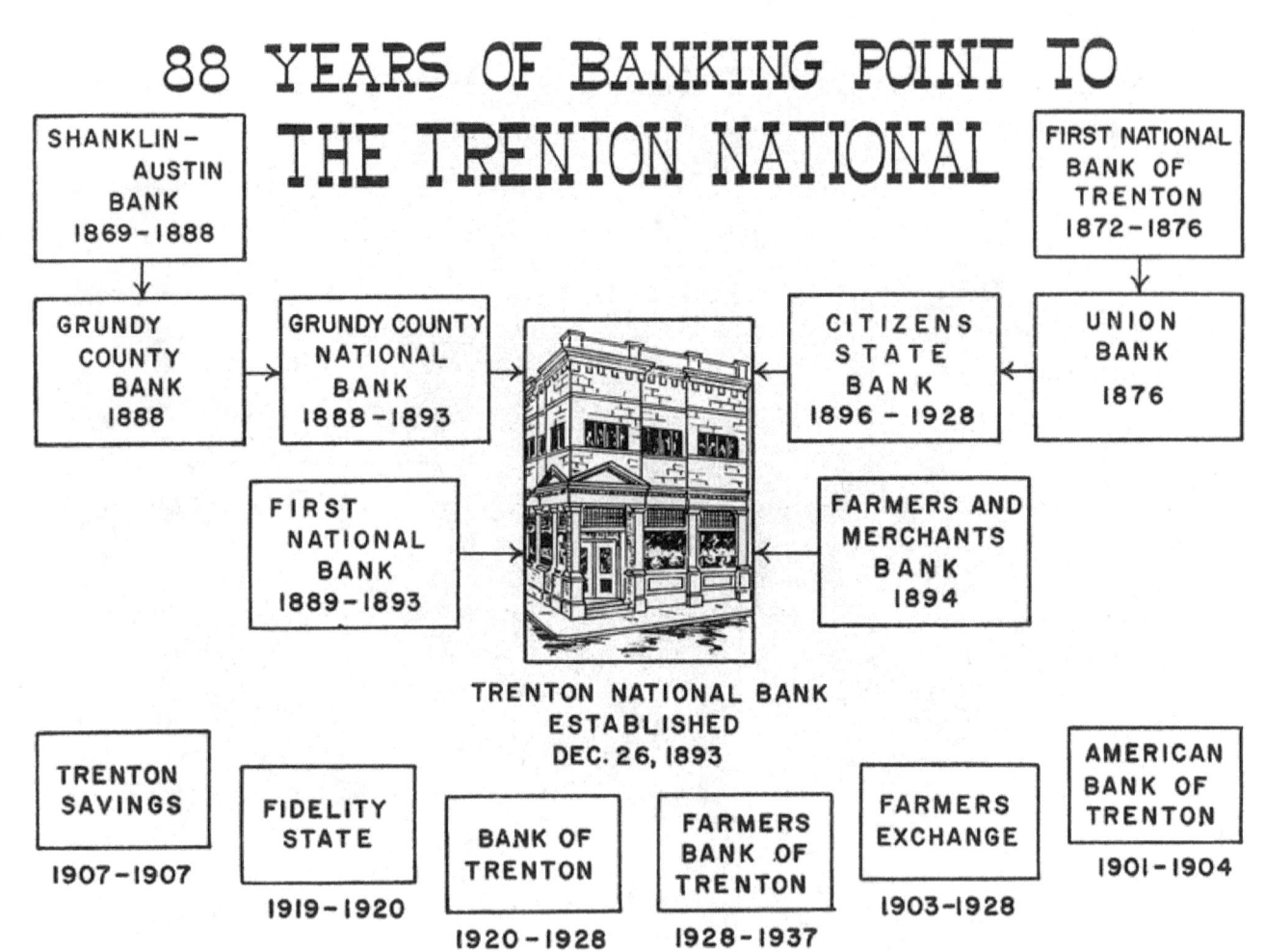

HOW BANKING STARTED IN TRENTON

Before the days of banks in Trenton, John H. Shanklin and James Austin operated a general merchandise store. As a service to their customers, they would keep their money in the store's safe, crediting additional sums to their accounts and debiting them with amounts withdrawn from time to time, Thus can be seen the development of the banking system, not only in Trenton, but elsewhere in the country. The first requisite was a safe place to keep the money-- and in the early days only a few business concerns owned safes. Those which did, such as the Shanklin-Austin Store, accommodated their customers by keeping their money for them. No charge was made for the service, as it drew more customers into the store.

At first no checks were written and all business was done in person. Later it was found expedient to send a note to the storekeeper telling him to pay "John Doe" a dollar for work he had done. As an ever increasing stream of "John Does" came into the store each day, the bookkeeping involved demanded more and more of the proprietor's time.

This is what happened to Messrs. Shanklin and Austin, for in 1869, they opened a private bank known as the Shanklin-Austin Bank with a five-thousand-dollar capital. The history of the Trenton National Bank begins with this early institution.

Through The Years, The Trenton National Bank Has Stayed Abreast Of The Times, Offering Today Every Modern Banking Facility

Since its establishment in 1893, the Trenton National Bank has shown a steady growth in deposits, reflecting the confidence of the community.

DEPOSITS

June 30, 1937	$1,207,522.24
June 30, 1939	$1,280,420.59
June 30, 1941	$1,419,677.15
June 30, 1943	$2,412,423.81
June 30, 1945	$3,978,598.77
June 30, 1947	$4,642,656.12
June 30, 1949	$4,364,741.81
June 30, 1951	$4,649,956.03
June 30, 1953	$5,674,414.34
June 30, 1955	$5,569,584.12
June 30, 1956	$5,745,667.46
Dec. 31, 1956	$6,503,535.61

BANK AND STAFF OF YESTERYEAR

LEFT TO RIGHT: Charles A. Mason, assistant cashier; Charles Herrin, bookkeeper; Walter H. Shanklin, cashier; W. E. Austin, Sr., president. Shanklin and Austin were sons of the founders of Trenton's first bank- the Shanklin-Austin Bank.

BANK AND STAFF TODAY

OUR STAFF OFFERS YOU COMPLETE, MODERN AND FRIENDLY BANKING SERVICE

LEFT TO RIGHT: G. A. Cullers, Ray V. Denslow, Jerrold L. Stuart, Harold C. Tracy, Wilbur E. Austin, Hugh C. Brummitt, Jack K. Ebbe, R. E. Cullers, Dr. C. H. Cullers.

BROTHERS OF THE BRUSH

LEFT TO RIGHT: Hazel Murphy, Barbara Skinner, Lillian Delameter, Mary Crow, Louise Gallatin, Jane Austin, Amy Morrison, Bernice Thomas, Mamie Williams, Betty Scott.

SISTERS OF THE SWISH

PROVEN DEPENDABILITY SINCE 1893

THE TRENTON NATIONAL BANK

Member Of The
Federal Reserve System

Member Of Federal Deposit
Insurance Corporation

Accounts Insured To $10, 000, 00

THE OLD - Where General Pershing Took His West Point Examinations.

In an act orgdnizing Grundy county January 29, 1841, the state legislature designated the house of James S. Lomax as the seat of the circuit and county court, and as such it has the title to the first courthouse in Grundy county. This storehouse, the first erected in the county, was built by James R. Devaul about 1838. It was a fine building for those days, built of hewn square logs, fitted nicely, and the plastering done with real lime mortar instead of mud, which was a decided innovation. After a short stay in the storehouse, the seat of justice was moved to the old log Baptist church where it remained until the first courthouse was built in 1842.

The contract for the first courthouse was let to William Collier and others of Howard county in March, 1842. William Collier later became a resident of Grundy county and was one of the most prominent citizens in the community. The old courthouse was a two-story brick building. The structure was located on the site of the present courthouse, block number two, fronting what was then Water street, being 30 feet from said street and also 30 feet from Trenton avenue. The structure measured 45x40 feet, had no basement, but a foundation dug below the surface of the ground. The balance of the wall was laid in Flemish brick 40 feet high to the roof of the second story. The contract further called for two doors and 21 windows, the entire structure to be surmounted by a "Gothick cupelo," 21 feet high, the base 13 feet square, and the dome covered with a thick tin. The cost of the building was $6,000.

For sixty years this little brick courthouse served the needs of the county, General Pershing took his West Point examinations within its walls in 1881, and later, General Crowder. An attempt was made to build a new courthouse in 1892, the proposition, however, was voted down. In the fall of 1901 the county court called a special election for December 10, 1901 for the purpose of voting on a new courthouse. The issue carried in every township save two by a vote of 1,970 to 588. The bonds were issued February 10, 1902, and sold to the Trenton National Bank at a premium of $1,200. The bond issue for $60,000 called for th e building of a jail as well as the courthouse.

EARLY RAILROAD

Trenton-Chillicothe Railroad: There are several places along the highway between Trenton and Chillicothe where the remains of this railroad can be seen-- a roadbed with neither ties nor rails, but to be real frank about it, it never did have ties or rails. For twenty years the hopes for a railroad between Trenton and Chillicothe rose and fell. It all started with the Chillicothe and Des Moines City railroad, when at that time the roadbed was made. When the company sold out to the Chicago & Southwestern, this stretch was abandoned for a route south through Gallatin.

THE NEW

Trenton's Part in The Civil War

G.A.R. Encampment
May 13, 14, 15-1908

The outbreak of the Civil War found Grundy in a peculiar position. In politics the county had been Democratic, so much in fact that only two or three votes had been cast for Lincoln. Many of the citizens were slave owners, and a great proportion of the settlers had migrated from the southern states. But the men of Grundy were not wont to take up arms against their constitutional government, and being in the northern part of a border state, they were not subjected to the cross currents of pressure and propaganda by the Confederacy.

In May, 1861, a singular occurrence took place- one which happened in very few places throughout the United States-meetings of both the Union and Confederate groups were held, each meeting being addressed by those favoring their respective causes. The Union meeting had the largest crowd by far, and from that day the Federalists gained strength and courage, gathering in the great numbers of undecided. The break was new made; Grundy county was with the Union.

There were no Confederate companies formed in this county, but about 200 men joined the South. A Captain Coleman recruited a few men here in 1861, but most of the 200 left in groups of from five to twenty and made their way south. Captain Jacob Bain, of Lincoln township, raised a company in Mercer county and came down to his old home in Lincoln where he recruited a number of his friends until the company numbered 183 men. They camped awhile at Edinburg and then went to Chillicothe where they were mustered in Col. Clark's regiment.

Mrs. Lowell B. Moore demonstrates the 1897 vintage telephone in operation.

Mrs. C. W. Chastain using the latest 1957 design in telephones which has been available for just a short time.

Telephone styles have changed - Has the conversation?

Grand River Mutual Telephone Corp.

Providing telephone service for Grundy County members around Galt, Laredo, Spickard and Brimson.

LEFT TO RIGHT: Paul Deskins, Mary Lee Coleman, Cecille Feurt, Leo Feurt, Harold Mason, Joe Bentley.

One of the older houses of Trenton was the present site of the Hub Cleaners.

Congratulations on

Trenton's 100 Years

HUB CLEANERS

Spanish-American War

GRUNDY COUNTY RECRUITS FOR THE SPANISH-AMERICAN WAR

Left to Right: Sgt. Lazorus, Lester Neville, Tib Coyle, Hugh Neville, Ed Brennenstuhl Geo. Ayres, Bert Bobinson, Unknown, Lon Mower, Ed Whitney, Britt Turner, Ike Holmes Tobe Huffman, Joe Michaels, Chas. Bates, Art Smith, Forrest Keene, R. L. Carscadin.

Cafe

Pool

Tavern

Trenton

Budweiser On Tap

Robert Keefe, Owner

Keefe's Recreation

Missouri

Gambles Congratulates Trenton
A Great Place to Live and to Work

Present personnel shown above are, Tom Hansbrough, Manager, Jim Griffith, Appliance Department Head, Dale Parker, Assistant Manager and Willia Gwinn, Office.

When considering Trenton's colorful 100 year history, Gambles is a comparative newcomer to this city. The first Gamble store in Trenton was opened on March 24th, 1934 at 909-911 Main Street.

Gamble-Skogmo was then a comparatively new organization. Just 9 years before two young men - Bertin C. Gamble and P. W. Skogmo - co-founded the organization by opening the first Gamble store in St. Cloud, Minnesota in March of 1925.

It was an auto supply store, popular with Sunday mechanics of the day whose hobby was "do-it-yourself" repairs on their Model "A" Fords. Friendly service was - and has continued to be - the policy. The store soon branched out into other lines of merchandise. such as hardware, paint and building supplies. The organization grew, and by 1928 there were 55 Gamble stores in the upper midwest.

The Gamble Authorized Dealer Plan was introduced in 1933. This plan offers the independent store owner an opportunity to enjoy planned success in a business of his own. Gamble's buying and warehousing facilities and merchandising know-how are put at the disposal of the individual, store owners. Although the Dealer Plan started during the depression, it caught on at once. Today there are over 1, 700 Gamble Authorized Dealers operating stores in 21 states. The company's Home Office is maintained at Minneapolis, Minnesota. Warehouses are centrally located to serve all stores in the organization.

In 1934 Gambles selected Trenton as a store site because of its progressive, stable economy. The Trenton Gamble store has enjoyed steady progress in merchandise sales as well as services to customers. It now features automotive, hardware, housewares, appliances, and sporting goods departments. March 12, 1954 - just 20 years after the store opened - it was burned out. Gambles operated at a temporary location while rebuilding on their original site at 909-911 Main Street.

Thomas Hansbrough, present manager of this store joins the entire Gamble organization in congratulating Trenton on its Centennial Celebration. The folks at Gambles are proud to be counted among the many fine merchants who serve the thousands of families in the Trenton area.

GAMBLE'S
"The Friendly Store"

"Co. D" and Other Trenton Boys Served Gallantly in World War I

Major W.C. Williamson who commanded "Co. D" had this to say about his outfit;

I dedicate these remarks to the best company of soldiers that ever got into a uniform, the most loyal group to their officers in the service, men whom I have never heard brag about what they accomplished, or protest any of the hardships which they endured.

It was one of the best drilled organizations in the service, and, as a whole, just a little better class of men than most organizations.

Their record proves they took advantage of all instructions given, for they took 185 men and three officers away, and returned with all but five. Many were wounded and gassed, and all of them injured physically, for no man can go through what they did and not suffer the penalty sooner or later. Many companies that did not see as much fighting as D, had five to ten times greater losses and more wounded. The men of Company D, were in the pink of condition physically and knew how to take care of themselves, or they never could have taken what they did in the trenches, and fight the exposures that are incident to the service, without any sickness. They left home as boys and came back as men; men of experience who were not afraid to shoulder responsibility.

Oyler's

Paint & Wallpaper Store

Years Ago it Took Days for Paint to Dry
But Now-Rubberized DaTex Wall Paint Dries in
Just 23 Minutes See Us For Every Modern Paint
Product-Paint Supplies and Latest Wallpapers
Also A Large Stock of Gifts and Housewares
Gifts - Housewares - Sundries
920 Main - Telephone 469
Trenton, Missouri

Roy Foster, Mgr.
George Taylor, Norman Baker
Joseph Murray

M. F. A.

Central Cooperative

Feed - Grain - Produce

Seed - Fertilizer

BOARD OF DIRECTORS AND EMPLOYEES: FRONT ROW: Left to Right: Geo. McGuire, Pete Dockery, Arrie McClaskey, A. G. Urton. BACK ROW: Francis Karr, john Longstreth, Robert Ishmael, R. B. Tharp, Gerald Sibbit, Herman Willis, S. M. Crawford.

The Peoples Co-Op Oil Co. started business in 1930, with 175 members at the same location that they now occupy at 3 02 E. 9th Street, Trenton, Missouri. The membership has increased through the years and in 1947, a new modern service station was built so that the members'could be given better service. The company handles Co-Op Petroleum Products, tires, batteries, paint, electric appliance's . Operates two tank wagons for farm deliveries and is the dealer for the Cockshutt Farm Machinery Co. in this territory.

The Peoples Co-Op Oil Co. is affiliated with Consumers Co-operative Association, Kansas City, Missouri.

PEOPLES CO-OP OIL CO .
Trenton, Missouri

Many Trenton and Grundy County Men
SERVED THEIR COUNTRY DURING WORLD WAR II

Their Gallant Service is Remembered in the Grundy County Honor Roll Erected in the Court House by the Trenton Lions Club.

Watch The "Birdie"
For Jerald

Our 20th Year

Juanita Worley, Ann Wright, Janice Vaughn

Wright Studio and Camera Shop

Your Centennial Photographer

BACK ROW: Dean Seidel, O. P. Nisbeth, Dorris Rider, Sam McGill, Bill Foster, Donald Cooksey, Bill Marshall, Bob Whorton, Willard McClallan. FRONT ROW: Chuck Timmons, John Prichett, Ernest Holloway, Ernest Ellington, Benford Tharp, George Huffstutter.

O. P. Nisbeth cameto Trenton and organized the NisbethChevrolet Co. in the fall of 1927. The original dealership was housed in the building that is standing at 611 1/2 Main. The new building, present site of Nisbeth's, was opened for business with the showing of the 1950 Model Car - 1957 marks his:

30th Year at 7th & Main

SALES  SERVICE

Used Cars-Trucks
Complete Mechanical and Body Service

NISBETH CHEVROLET CO.

Grand River College

GRUNDY COUNTY'S FIRST VENTURE IN HIGHER EDUCATION

During the first one hundred years, there have been five established colleges in Grundy county; Grand River College, Avalon College, Ruskin College, Trenton College, and the present junior college. At one time Grundy county was the acknowledged seat of learning in northwest Missouri. Today a very high degree of literacy prevails, thanks to our forefathers who were wise enough to lay the groundwork.

Grand River College was the first institution of higher learning in the county and probably has the most romantic history. It was organized at Edinburg, August, 1850; the building was constructed by a Mr. Edgar, a quarter of a mile north of the later location. Here the first co-educational movement in the State of Missouri had its beginning. It was incorporated February 27, 1851.

I. B. Allen was the founder and John O. Martin the first teacher, with Mrs. Anne Bryan as associate.

At th e beginning of the second year, Professor John Ordway, of Massachusetts, became the principal of the school and Mr. M. McKean and Miss Flora Belle Chamberlin were added as assistants. One hundred students were now enrolled. On Christmas day, 1853, fire broke out from a defective flue and the building was destroyed, ending the career of the Old Grand River Academy.

For a period of five years Grand River Academy was just a memory, but in 1858, John T. Witten and William Peery became interested in the reorganization of the school and with the help of Dr. John Cullers, then a representative in the legislature, they obtained a charter from that body, February 28, 1859.

Grand River College was the first school west of the Mississippi to open its doors to females. A pioneer in the field of education, it will long be remembered for that fact alone. Mrs. Anne E. Bryan was the first female teacher, and at the dedication of the old college on November 30, 1850, she delivered an eloquent plea for co-education.

EMPLOYEES: FRONT ROW: Frank Hoffman, Hugh Johnson, Darlene Dean, Dora Ellis, Ivory Kincaid, Nadene Harris, Lloyd Crow, Mont Johnson. BACK ROW: Harold Brewer, Wendell Lent, Bill Mullins, Clifford. Stevens, Bill Stubbs, Richard Crawford, Charles D. Hoffman.

We were not here 100 years ago but hope to be here for the next 100.

This business was started 1945 by E. B. Moore and purchased 1950 by the present owners: Charles D. Hoffman, Charles D. Reed, and H. Frank Hoffman. It was started as a feed, seed, fertilizer, produce and farm supply store, and has since added a new modern grain elevator.

The business has been built on service and serving you is our goal.

Congratulations Trenton on your first 100 years.

HOFFMAN & REED FARM SUPPLY STORE

Other Colleges in Trenton

Ruskin College

Grundy county was the seat of one of the first socialistic movements in the state. Not exactly the same "ism" as we know today, but what its leaders termed "Christian socialism." Mr. and Mrs. Walter Vrooman were the founders of the "Multitude Incorporated" of which Ruskin College was the central institution. The Vroomans, reputedly wealthy, were possessed with the humanitarian desire to change the form of the body politic, and believing that most institutions of higher learning looked favorably on the capitalistic system, conceived the idea of establishing their own college.

Ruskin College began its career September, 1900, as the Central College for America of the Ruskin Hall Educational System, established by Mr. and Mrs. Walter Vrooman at Oxford, England, February 22, 1898. The English institution had secured an enrollment of three thousand in less than three years. Their first move in Missouri was to buy the Avalon College building, that institution having ceased operation the year before. Next, the college bought 1,800 acres of land, and engaged the services of Professor H. M. Cottrel, formerly superintendent of Governor Levi P. Morton's great farm at Rhinecliff on the Hudson, and later Professor of Agriculture in the State Agricultural College of Kansas, to superintend the farm. Many students were employed here, and it was expected to develop a large dairy herd, the profits from which would practically support the school.

The school fared quite well for several years, having in 1902 representatives from Alaska, California, Colorado, Illinois, New York, Pennsylvania, Indiana, Iowa, Kansas, Kentucky, Missouri, Massachusetts, Minnesota, New Jersey, New Mexico, Nebraska, Ohio, Oklahoma Territory, Oregon, Texas, and several foreign countries, although the main body of students were from Missouri, especially Grundy county. Two degrees-- Bachelor of Arts and Master of Accounts (business course)--were conferred.

Avalon College

In April, 1869, the Missouri Mission Conference of the Church of the United Brethren in Christ withdrew its support of Lane University, Kansas, after receiving poor treatment there, and voted to establish an academy within its own bounds.

The board, after a short deliberation as to the location, chose "Scott's Mound," Fairview township, Livingston county, Missouri.

On July 24, 1890, the board voted to move the college to Trenton. F. A. Z. Kumler was the mainspring of the movement. Halls were rented and work began September 15, 1890. Without one cent of help from church or town, President Kumler ran a successful school with a first-year enrollment of 308.

To raise the money for the college, a farm was purchased adjoining the east side of the city, streets laid our, and the subdivided land sold to public spirited citizens for $40,000. A fine three-story brick building was erected for $30,000. It had twenty-nine rooms. It was erected in the center of the addition where the high school now stands. It was lighted with electricity and gas, and heated with steam.

Five degrees were conferred by the college: Bachelor of Arts, Bachelor of Science, Bachelor of Pedagogy, Master of Arts, and Master of Science. In addition to the regular academic courses, one department was termed the "Business Institute" and was further subdivided into theory and practice departments.

Frances Speir, . Jennie Hoover
Beulah Herndon

The Latest Fashions & Accessories For
Tots - Sub-Teens - Jr.
Boys' Wear - Infants to 8 yrs.
Maternity Dept.

The Toggery Shop

LEFT TO RIGHT: Lois Dale, Mony Powell, Glenn Stickler, Frances Warren, J. M. Dale.

We try to make this a store of real service---to be helpful to you in a practical way, whether you come seeking a gift, something for yourself, your home, to have repair work done or simply to look around.

We are your FRANCHISED DEALER for the following:

STERLING SILVER

Towle   Gorham   Wallace   International   Heirloom   Lunt

CHINA

Spode   Flintridge   Syracuse   Royal Titteau   Vernonware

CRYSTAL

Tiffin   Fostoria   Imperial   Duncan Miller   Bryce Bros.   Lotus

WATCHES

Longines   Wittnauer   Elgin   Bulova   Hamilton   High Grade Swiss

DIAMONDS

Feature Lock   Art Carved   "Stones set while you wait."

North Missouri's Finest Jewelry And Gift Store Since 1878
905 Main   Phone 406
Trenton, Missouri

Trenton Junior College

HIGHER EDUCATION STRONG IN TRENTON AT THE CENTENNIAL YEAR

The Trenton Junior College was organized primarily to meet the needs of the high school graduates in Trenton and the surrounding communities. The high school diploma did not mean much more at that time than did the eighth grade diploma twenty years earlier. That the number of college students in the state of Missouri had doubled during the years 1919 to 1924, was sufficient evidence that something needed to be done to meet the local demand for the higher work in education. In 1924, fifty-seven students had gone from Grundy county to various colleges, and the superintendent had a long list of those who desired to do so, but could not finance it.

The new college opened September 7, 1925, with an initial enrollment of sixty-five students, seventeen of the men reporting for football the same day.

In its second year, the enrollment jumped to 100 students and the following teachers were employed: Mary Guthrie, English; Z. T. Walter, chemistry and mathematics; Maude Woodruff, education; Jerry Lewis, coach; Mary Ann McDonald, music; Max Van Horn, biological science; Mrs. Anna Lyle Hill, social science; and Mary Ella Steckman, Spanish and English.

The first student council was composed of George Zeigler, Lex K. Souter, Russell Smith, Wilma Fortney, Mary Leeper, Kathryn Hulen, L. F. King, and I. L. Ebbe. March 31, 1927, the junior college bill passed the state legislature, under which all junior colleges were allowed to become part of the public school system, and March 2, 1928, the junior college was incorporated into the Trenton school system.

The first class, twenty-eight in number, was graduated in the spring of 1927. They were: Anna Armbruster, Ruth Lee Arnold, Edith Ball, Jeanette Bayne, Lenore Berneking, Lockie Lee Cannady, Ada Mae Cox, Harrell Davis, Wynema Ellis, George Fickinger, Wilma Fortney, Maurice Goins, Leola Harris, John Hemley, Kathryn Hulen, Wenona Kennedy, LaVerne Kerns, Merno King, Willa Ruth Knedler, Mary Leeper, Wilford Lowe, Virgil Muse, Madeline Price, Miriam Reed, Theodore Shields, Russell Smith, Lex King Souter.

Brown Shoe Fit Co.

11 Years in Trenton Retailing Shoes, Hosiery and Rubber Footwear

For The Entire Family

DONOHO'S HOME FURNISHINGS

DEPENDABLE QUALITY HOME FURNISHINGS AT REASONABLE PRICES
SINCE 1935 - YOU CAN "GUY WITH CONFIDENCE"
AT DONOHO'S

Since our beginning in 1935 we have enjoyed a growing business in this fine community. In these 22 years you people have given us a reputation that we work hard to preserve and build, a reputation of which we are very proud.

Honest and fair treatment to every customer's needs, unequalled service on all products we sell, and expert, skilled installation of carpeting, tile, and linoleum is our continued pledge.

We are anxious to serve you and your families. We invite you to visit our store at anytime, look around and make yourself at home at DONOHO'S HOME FURNISHINGS.

Trenton Schools

BRAINERD SCHOOL - TRENTON

In 1838, an Englishman by the name of Moore opened the first school to be taught in Trenton. The house was a rough log cabin located on the present site of the old cemetery. In 1839 the school was taken over by Jarvis Boyce who taught until 1841, then George H. Hubbell taught the winter of 1842-43. The first schools were conducted on the subscription plan, the teacher, who was generally a man, making from fifteen to eighteen dollars a month. His mental and educational equipment was often very meager, and as in later times, some teachers were more successful in making impressions on the back than on the mind. Now and then, however, an ambitious young man of culture who was seeking his fortune in the new country would start by teaching a few terms of school. Reading, writing, spelling and arithmetic constituted the course of study. Any unreasonable desire for more learning was gratified by going further in arithmetic. The teacher, who had been through fractions, was a very learned man.

The early schoolhouse was built of hewn logs, generally fourteen to eighteen feet square. A fireplace took a large part of one end of the room, the chimney was made of sticks and clay, the roof of clapboards, and kept in place by the weight of poles. Often on a windy day the boys would be excused to replace the poles and a section of roof. Individual desks were unheard-of luxuries. A long board, fastened against the wall slantwise, and held in place by pegs, was the writing desk, and the pupils would line up to it in a row for penmanship instruction. Two small windows with oiled paper for panes usually furnished the light, but sometimes the more simple method of leaving a log out of the side was resorted to. Log schoolhouses were not uncommon as late as 1880.

In 1844, a system of public schools was inaugurated in Trenton and a school board chosen; the board, in turn, elected Colonel Jacob Tindall to take charge of the school. In 1853, D. T. Wright, of his own means, erected the first frame building in the county for school purposes, and the school was brought from the graveyard to town, with Mr. Wright as teacher. In the meantime, judge Snyder had driven all the church organizations from the courthouse where they had been accustomed to hold services, and the school building was rented by the various denominations, as it was the only available place to hold services.

In 1855, Joseph Ficklin opened a school in a log house on the site of the present jail. Ficklin, later, was a professor of mathematics in the state university. In the same year, Terrence Bradley opened a school, and was such a popular teacher that more room was needed to accommodate his students; consequently, he built a two-story building where the Farmer's Store stood, now occupied by Montgomery and Ward. Mr. Bradley died in 1860, and the unfinished term was filled by his wife. The first music department was added to this school and taught by Miss Chamberlin (later Mrs. J. O. Harris). Then followed the dark period of history, for all phases of life were neglected during the war days. A Mr. Colley and L. Collier were in charge of the school until 1863, when Professor R. C. Norton came from Ohio to take over the system.

POST WAR SCHOOLS

The first high school was organized in Trenton by R. C. Norton on September 18, 1865, with twenty-three pupils. Professor Norton had conducted his school in the old district schoolhouse from 1863 to 1865, but when the enrollment increased to twenty-three in that year, he organized the first high school in the Bradley building. But students kept coming until soon that building was outgrown and a larger one became necessary. In 1868 the number of pupils was 150, and the total cost for the year $1,480.

A high school building was erected in the year 1870, by W. H. Smith contractor, at a cost of $15,000,

Fisher-Meeker Furniture Co.

1322-24-26 Main   Phone 57

Trenton Schools

NORTON SCHOOL - TRENTON

half in cash and half in school bonds. The building was located on what at that time was "a gentle knoll in the resident portion of the city, well located and convenient in all its appliances". The junior high building now occupies that spot. The building itself was of two-story brick construction, seventy feet square. At this time the high school employed four teachers, R. C. Norton, high school; B. F. Thomas, grammar department; Miss Bell Rozell, primary; and Mrs. Hattie Robertson, painting and drawing. An advertisement was carried in the papers of surrounding counties soliciting the at-

TRENTON JUNIOR HIGH SCHOOL

tendance of students at two dollars a month for high school, and a dollar and a half for grammar school. In 1870, the year the new building was completed, 370 pupils were enrolled; in 1871 the enrollment was 532, and in 1885 it was 1,414.

Professor Norton served as the first superintendent of Trenton schools from 1865 to 1875 when he resigned to accept a position at the Warrensburg State Normal, despite the fact that his salary was raised from $800 to

(Continued On Page 76)

CLAUDIA'S

At Claudia's you'll find quality plus style at prices you can afford to pay.

Under New Management 1 Year
Mrs. Claudia Mapes, Owner

Mrs. Martha Oberg
21 Years As An Employee

Maid-Rite Cafe

Good Food Year Around

Since 1946

Trenton Lodge No. III A. F. & A. M. IS EIGHT YEARS OLDER THAN TRENTON

Oldest of the secret societies is the Freemasons, and naturally it was first to be established in Grundy county. The first record of the meeting of any secret society in the county is the record of the meeting held October 10, 1849, for the purpose of forming a lodge of Freemasons, later to be chartered as Trenton Lodge No. 111 A.F. & A. M., which has had a continuous organization since that date. In 1870,. there was organized a chapter of Royal Arch Masons; in 1874, a commandery of Knights Templar, and in 1920, a council of Royal and Select Masters, thereby completing the full series of degrees which comprise the York Rite of Freemasonry.

Trenton Lodge was organized by virtue of a dispensation issued September 25, 1849, by the D.D.G.M., B. F. Atwood of Carrollton. Rev. Isaac B. Allen was named in the dispensation as Master, Benj. H. Smith as Senior Warden, and B. S. Nordyke as Junior Warden. Allen was the first president of Grand Riser College and Smith was later to serve as the first president of Culver-Stockton College. The first place of meeting is said to have been in the home of Bro. Nordyke; later the lodge rented a room in Tracy's Tavern, located just south of the courthouse block. The lodge has had various meeting places during its ninety years of existence. At one time the meetings were held in the grand jury room of the old courthouse. Later we find them in the buildings at the southwest corner of 7th and Main, northwest corner of 8th and Main, northwest corner of 11th and Main, and then in 1895, to the new hall at 811 1/2 Main, where they have met ever since.

TRENTON CHAPTER 66, R.A.M.

A chapter of this branch of Masonry was organized July 14, 1870, under a dispensation issued to the late Governor A. M. Dockery on June 30, 1870. Applicants for the dispensation were Marshall Fulton, Dr. J. E. Harris, Wm. Pond, S. C. Loveland, N. A. Winters, Rich. F. Keith, J. L. Shipley, W. W. Brooks, and Stephen B. Bank. A charter was issued October 6, 1870, to the above named petitioners and to A. H. Burkeholder, James H. Kerfoot, Stephen Peery, Wm. H. Roberts, and A. K. Sykes; Fulton, Harris, and Pond were the first three officers under dispensation and under charter.

The first Royal Arch Mason in Grundy county was undoubtedly Dr. Joseph E. Harris, who went horseback to Huntsville, Mo., in 1855 and there received the degrees of the chapter in Huntsville Chapter No. 13, now defunct. By 1870, the membership of the parent body in Trenton was large enough to justify the coming of this popular branch of the fraternity and within a few years the membership had grown very large.

TRENTON COUNCIL NO. 37, R.S.M.

This branch of Freemasonry was long neglected in this territory, although offering more in the way of a study of Masonic symbolism than many other degrees. In the beginning, most Grundy county Masons journeyed to Milan, Mo., where they received these degrees; then came a period when councils began to travel over north Missouri and confer the degrees in lodge halls. Previous to 1915, Ray V. Denslow and James H. Clawson were the only two Trentonites known to possess these degrees. In 1915, Solomon Council came to Trenton and conferred the degrees on Dr. James B. Wright, A. C. Gwinn, Platt Hubbell, R. E. Kavanaugh, D. F. Warren, Jas. T. Carnes, Harry L. Asher, John R. Merrill, Carl Albrektsen, John R. Kernahan, O. E. Martin, A. E. Fouts, Chas. A. Collier, Oliver H. Faus, F. M. McKinney. Other classes were held in 1917, 1918 and 1919.

Because of the growing membership, and the inaccessibility of Milan at that time, the demand grew for a council in Trenton, and in reply to a petition addressed to Louis Moller, then Grand Master, a dispensation was issued August 7, 1920, authorizing them to form a Council which was later given the name of Trenton Council No. 37, R. & S.M..

GODFREY DE BOUILLON COMMANDERY

Godfrey de Bouillon Commandery No. 24, Knights Templar, was organized May 21, 1874, when John Ure, Grand Commander, in response to a petition, issued a dispensation to James C. Wyatt, E. R. Fetherstonh, A. D. Mullins, J. B. Farnam, W. H. McGrath, Thos. Kimlin, H. J. Herrick, J. H. Kerfoot, and R. O. Carscadin, authorizing them to form a commandery under the above name in the city of Trenton. All of the above petitioners came with dimits from the commandery at Brookfield, with the exception of J. B. Farnam, who had a dimit from Eureka Commandery No. 3, in Michigan. Wyatt, Fetherstonh and Mullins were the first three principal officers.

The first manbers knighted were T. M. Hall, John Kirk, J. L. Nichols, Isaac M. Patton, W. H. Roberts, George Tindall; later were added J. M. Bailey, A. H. Burkeholder, C. C. Parker and Thos. Hilton. On November 21, 1878, P. G. Commander, Geo. W. Belt

(Continued On Page 155)

LEFT TO RIGHT: Alfred Routh, Leon Trump, Wes Applegate, Murk Mahaffie.

GRUNDY COUNTY LUMBER CO.

Our business has been in continuous existence for more than half of the Centennial Year, and the Grundy County Lumber Co. has been under the management of Murk Mahaffie since 1929.

While fifty years ago a lumber yard was very much what the name indicated—its stocks confined to lumber and kindred items. It now furnishes practically all the materials needed in construction.

The Grundy County Lumber Co. has appreciated the patronage it has received from the citizens of Trenton and Grundy County, and it is most happy to join in this Centennial celebration.

The Centennial Year MARKS A PERIOD OF GOOD STREETS IN TRENTON.
THIS WAS HARDLY SO IN 1916.

Laclede Street looking toward the Rock Island Depot and the "Beanery."

LEFT TO RIGHT Maurice D. Pond, son of Mr. and Mrs. Harold Pond, Mrs. Judson M. Morrison, daughter of Mr. and Mrs. Pond, Cheryl Lynn Morrison, granddaughter, Harold Pond, Debra Kay Morrison, granddaughter, Mrs. Harold Pond, Mrs. Barbara Proctor, bookkeeper.

LEFT TO RIGHT: Maurice Pond, John Reed, Sr., Harold Pond, D. H. Seymour, John Junior Reed.

Grand River Press

HAROLD POND,

811 MAIN STREET

MAURICE POND, Owners

Lee Shepard   Jack Brittain   Jimmy Dennis
John Adams Kelley Stottlemyre Hattie Robinson Dick Dean Nevin Adams

"To Give Service" - - -

More than a Motto---The Settled Policy Of This Firm

The Sincere Endeavor of Each Employee-
To Help Preserve the American Way of Life-
To Keep Our Faith In America's Agriculture-
To Hold Fast The Traditions Of Our Forefathers-
To Brighten The Pathway Of Those We Serve-
To Better Serve Our God, Our Country and Our Fellowman.

HOOVER & ADAMS

John Deere Quality Farm Equipment

1103 Tinsman Avenue   Phone 800

A FINE GROUP OF GRADUATES FROM Trenton H ugh School 1896:

BACK ROW: Left to Right:
Harry Hale
Ella Hart
Alice   Stamper
Carrie Walker
Ethel Shanklin Brown
Cosby Bailey Bowbon
Edith Debolt
Kate Pringle
Clifford   DeBois
2ND ROW:
Bessie Evans
Minnie   Robertson
Jessie Pelton
Nellie Carnes Kircher
Mildred   Phillips   Hausam
Rinds Greenabaum
Ida Lilly
FRONT ROW:
Judson Bain
Ralph Conrads
E. M. Bainter (teacher)
Clyde Phillips
Willis   Millington
Bert Woodruss

To Be Of Service ...
Is Man's Greatest Earthly Responsibility

Slater Funeral Home

Ambulance Service   Donald H. Slater   612 E. 9th St.

TOP ROW: Left to Right: V. Burkeybile, G. House, L. Noe, T. White, D. Critten, D. Egeland, M. Gardner, O. Fox, L. Long, V. Lovell, G. Shipley, J. Hutchison, T. R. Bass, superintendent. FRONT ROW. B. Binney, D. Page, D. Fuller, G. Sawyer, B. Hamilton, L. Christy, K. Soper.

DAVISON CHEMICAL CO.

Davison Chemical Company, Div. of W. R. Grace & Company was officially opened August 9, 1952. Its rated capacity is 25,000 tons of mixed granulated fertilizer a year. This plant serves Missouri and Southern Iowa. From 15 to 25 men are employed.

The First Railroad in Trenton

The railroad fever broke out again in 1864, even before the close of the Civil war. This time it assumed proportions that gave hope that the iron horse might come snorting over the prairies and woodlands of the county in triumph. The Chillicothe & Des Moines City, which changed to Chicago & Southwestern, and still later to the Chicago, Rock Island & Pacific, was the first road to take practical shape and to promise gratifying results. In 1864 a charter was procured for the Brunswick & Chillicothe railroad (now the Wabash), followed by the Chillicothe & Des Moines railway the next year. It was the design that the people of Iowa should cooperate in the movement to obtain a railroad from the capital, south through the Grand river country, via Brunswick to St. Louis.

Accordingly, on April If, 1868, a special election was held and the proposition to subscribe $200,000 was carried by more than a two-thirds vote.

Steps were at once taken to employ a corps of engineers to locate the road and early in June, 1868, a large force was put to work to survey the road, with Peter Markey as chief and H. N. Armstrong as assistant engineer. This work was pressed vigorously, so that as early as the 10th of February, 1869, the road was ready to be let for construction; on that date the contract for grading, bridging and tieing the road from Chillicothe to Princeton, a distance of 49 miles, was awarded to Noland & Moore for $320,000 in bonds of the company, which proved to be insufficient. The construction of the roadbed was commenced at once and pushed vigorously until July, when a rainy season set in and almost totally stopped the work, and as no contract for ironing, equipping and operating the road up to this time had been obtained, the spirit of criticism was developed and considerable opposition manifested itself against the further issuing of county bonds in payment of its subscription, which at this time amounted to approximately $50,000.

CHICAGO & SOUTHWESTERN AND ROCK ISLAND

In February, 1870, negotiations were opened between the Chillicothe & Des Moines and the Chicago & Southwestern Railroad companies, which on April 20, 1870, resulted in an agreement as follows: That the Chillicothe & Des Moines company let and lease to the Chicago & Southwestern company all that portion of the roadbed between Princeton and Trenton, and such further portion south of Trenton as might be necessary to, make a convenient crossing of the east fork of Grand river, for the full term of nine hundred and ninety nine years, on the condition that the lessees should, within eighteen months from that time, iron and operate the road. This contract was put in writing on June 3, 1870. The Chicago & Southwestern railroad was a mere construction company backed and indorsed by the Chicago, Rock Island & Pacific, which was the real party interested in finding an outlet to the Missouri River.

LOCATING THE MACHINE SHOPS

When the tracklayers were nearing the Grundy county line, the optimism of the people rose to a new level and on June 8, 1871, a meeting was held at the courthouse for the purpose of getting an expression from the citizens of Trenton in relation to offering inducements to the C. &S.W. railroad to locate their machine shops and roundhouse at this point. A week later the newspaper carried the jubilant news that the tracklayers had crossed the Mercer and Grundy line a few minutes before 9 o'clock Wednesday, June 14, 1871, and still were pushing their way toward Trenton, undoubtedly arriving in twelve more days. The committee appointed to locate the machine shops bored in two places for water and found sufficient in both places for a machine shop; therefore, the city council on July 6 ordered the issuance of ten bonds of one thousand dollars each to mature in ten years for the location of the shops in Trenton. In addition to this, the company received about $3,000 worth of land and $50,000 in eight per cent bonds from the town of Trenton. The bonds had been voted as early as July, 1869, when it was suggested that the road might pass through Trenton.

On July 2, 1885, the machine shops caught fire and the building and equipment were destroyed completely. Three engines were removed from the shops with much

Rock Island Machine Shops Located in Trenton

difficulty. The loss was estimated at $125,000 and none if it was covered by insurance. The greatest loss, however, was experienced by the 100 men who were thrown out of work.

In the year 1885, the Rock Island began construction on a line to St. Joseph, Missouri. Passenger trains were run from Atchison, Kansas, to Trenton via St. Joseph and, upon their arrival here, the through trains were made up. This gave Trenton two more passenger trains a day. The first shipment which was made over the new line from Maysville on December 8, 1885, consisted of seven cars of stock which were shipped east to St. Joseph junction and thence over the main line to Kansas City. By February, 1886, the trains were giving service to Trenton, the first one arriving on the tenth of that month with four carloads of hogs shipped from Amity, one of the new stations.

The first "fast train" made its run on December 28, 1887, making the record run of three hours and forty minutes between Kansas City and Trenton and the people congregated at every station along the route to see the train fly past.

The Rock Island, as originally planned and built, did not enter Kansas City, but crossed the Missouri at St. Joseph. Later, as Kansas City grew in importance, the Rock Island entered into an arrangement with the Burlington railroad, under which Rock Island trains entered Kansas City by using the Burlington tracks between Cameron Junction and Birmingham, Missouri, a distance of 44 miles. The distance was long and the curves and grades of the track were unfavorable. In order to shorten the distance, improve the grades and obtain more favorable curvature, the Rock Island constructed its own line from Hickory Creek to Nettleton. Construction of this new line commenced in July, 1929, on the Hickory Creek-Nettleton section and in April, 1930, on the Nettleton-Birmingham section, and the line was finished and in operation by September 27, 1931.   The total cost was $14,200,000. The new line, because of improved grades and curves, permitted operating economies by making possible the handling of longer trains and by the shortening of the distance. An arrangement was made with the Chicago, Milwaukee, St. Paul and Pacific for the joint use of their line between Polo and Birmingham as a second main line, giving double track facilities to that territory. The route over the new line was 8.54 miles shorter than the former route.

Trenton Livestock Market & East Side Lumber Yard

Trenton Livestock Market the place to receive full market price for your livestock and whatever you have to sell.

We also operate the East Side Lumber Yard. The place to fill your building and fencing needs. Our motto - Good Service.

The "O K" Railroad

TRENTON'S SECOND MAJOR LINE IN 1881

CEASED OPERATION IN 1939

DO YOU REMEMBER CONRAD ROSE, OUR GERMAN TAILOR?

He could tell a serious story in the most hilarious manner. It appears he gave $100.00 to put the OK Railroad through, and on the day of completion was at hand. He reported this eventful day, "Veil, I vendt down to see de furst train come in, and vat do you tink? De furst man to get off vas a new tailor"?

In the year of 1873, Madison township voted down a proposition to subscribe $25,000 to the Quincy, Missouri & Pacific, and Marion township carried a like proposition while Trenton township voted $50,000 to the road at the same town. On the 22nd of October, 1875, Marion township voted $15,000 more. Numerous propositions were voted upon and carried and had the company been able to come west a few years sooner, it would have obtained several thousand dollars more than it received finally. The progressive spirit which had all along governed the people of Trenton township was exhibited toward the "0. K." as toward the first.

The arrival of the first Rock Island train spurred the people on and two days afterwards on Saturday, September 30, 1871, a large and enthusiastic meeting was held to consider the propriety of another railroad. One had been obtained, why not another? A committee was appointed to confer with the officers of the Quincy, Missouri & Pacific Railroad with reference to suggesting a preliminary survey of said road via Lindley, Trenton and Edinburg in Grundy county, Col. J. H. Shanklin was elected chairman and W. H. Roberts, secretary. The committee found there was a good chance of the railroad being located in Grundy county if the citizens supported it.

The long-looked-for Quincy, Missouri & Pacific Railway, due at Trenton, July 1, 1881, by 12 o'clock midnight, arrived about sundown. The force of tracklayers had worked incessantly for some days, a double force being necessary to accomplish the work on time, and so they had pushed it night and day. They were greeted on their arrival by more than 2,000 people, with their shouts and the incessant scream of five whistles. While the citizens rejoiced there was no less rejoicing on the part of the railroad company, for the time specified to arrive' here having been accomplished, they were entitled to a private subscription of $40,000 which was given them as a bonus. The last spike was driven at 7:15 o'clock in the evening and five engines were on the track ready to close up the depot already completed. A coach, conveying the officers of the road from Quincy, was in the rear and was switched off on a sidetrack. When the almost unearthly scream of the whistles ceased and the crowd had become quiet, Dr. E. F. Horton stepped to the front and made a short speech of welcome, which was answered by Hon. W. G. Ewing, a lawyer of Quincy, in behalf of the company. Mr. Ewing praised the Quincy, Missouri & Pacific Company, the Wabash Company and the people of Trenton, referring among other things, to the band which had given $150 of its funds to aid in financing the road. After the speeches were made, the company rolled out twenty kegs of beer to the hands who had worked so hard to finish the road.

Prior to 1897, Trenton was the western terminus of this road, but in that year the lines of the Quincy, Omaha & Kansas City, as it was then called, were extended to Pattonsburg, making connections to Omaha and Kansas City. It was then under the control of the Wabash Company, which later sold out to the Burlington lines. On May 20, 1938, this company asked permission of the Interstate Commerce Commission to abandon its entire line extending from Quincy to Kansas City, a distance of 250 miles, but when the application precipitated a flood of protests, a new application superseding the old one was filed November 3, 1938, requesting permission to abandon the line between Milan, Missouri, and Kansas City, a distance of 143 miles.

The McVay Motor Company was founded in the year 1914 by Don C. McVay in Trenton, Missouri. In 1923 the company moved into its present location, 201 East Ninth Street.

Don McVay had been a Ford Dealer for 40 years when he passed away August 26, 1955.

The present McVay Motor Company, the Ford Car and Truck and Ford Tractor and Implement Dealer in Trenton, is owned by Jerrold Stuart, and the seventeen employees of the company are pictured below.

FRONT ROW: Left to Right; Ernest Kinnison, R. G. Cox, George Watts, Floyd Bosley, Elaine May, Agnes Lankford, Charles Giles, Dolph Kinnison, Russell Ratliff. BACK ROW: John Carter, Burnis Shepard, Victor Meeker, Charles Gott, Jerrold Stuart, Leroy Trobough, Charles Ingraham, Troy Lehr.

McVAY MOTOR COMPANY

FRONT ROW: Left to Right: R. V. Gilluly, Secretary; R. McAllister, Leading Knight; M. Bonta, Loyal Knight; D. Walker, Trustee. BACK ROW: R. W. Browning, Chaplain; F. Karr, Treasurer; W. J. Foster, Exalted Ruler; H. P. Hurst, Tiler; F. Mosier, Trustee; K. Elyea, Lecturing Knight.

Trenton Lodge No. 801, B. P. O. E.

For many years Trenton lacked a lodge exemplifying the purely social side of lodge work; on July 2, 1902, a few representative Trenton men passed around a papa, which; was signed by thirty-eight men desirous of becoming members of the Benevolent and Protective Order of Elks. That same night, a meeting was held in the Hotel Peery, where arrangements for organization were perfected and temporary officers elected.

On Tuesday evening August 5, 1902, the charter members of Trenton Lodge No. 801 were initiated into the mysteries of Elkdom at the Masonic Hall, with the work put on by the Chillicothe lodge of Elks. There were nearly fifty candidates in the new lodge and about the same number of visitors.

On August 14, 1902, the Trenton lodge was duly chartered by the Grand Lodge of the Benevolent and Protective Order of Elks of the United States of America. The first candidate initiated, after the lodge was organized, was James T. Carnes, on September 22, 1902. The first officers were follows: Charles D. Morris, Exalted Ruler; E. M. Harber, Esteemed Leading Knight; Hugh C. Smith, Esteemed Loyal Knight; H. J. Bain, Esteemed Lecturing Knight; T. F. Fulkerson, Esquire; C. J. Bain, Secretary; S. S. Day, Treasurer; E. G. Kathan, Inner Guard; B. J. McGuire, Tiler; R. M. Cook, C. J. Ringe, and W. A. Moore, Trustees.

One of the Winners IN THE ELKS PICNIC OF 1910 PARADE

LEFT TO RIGHT: Lucy Crooks, Vera Asher Meredith, Hazel Moonaw Kenderdine, Blanche Shanklin Brown.

LEFT TO RIGHT: Mrs. Roy Leeper, Mrs. Harold Brown, Owner; Mrs. Fern Spencer, Mrs. Frank Slonecker and Mrs. Sherman Cox.

STYLES REFLECT THE TIMES - YOU'LL FIND ONLY THE LATEST WHEN YOU SHOP AT

BROWN'S

922 MAIN   TRENTON, MISSOURI

The Elks Put on "The White Elephant",

The cast under the direction of Mr. and Mrs. J. A. Darnaby at the Hubbell Theater. FRONT ROW: Ray Preston, Gladys Jones, Florence Pringle, Frankie Cox, DeEtta Cox, Dora Jones, Mary Dennis, Lloyd Austin, Mildred Patton, Anna Melvin, Myrtle Davis, Helen Murphy. BACK ROW: Lela Schooler, Bain Fleming, Kent Sykes, George Carnes, Lems Pratt, Chas. Mason, Jewett Carnes, Walter Reel, Wilbur Austin, Dr. Collins, Austin Carnes, Ray Denslow, Helen Murphy.

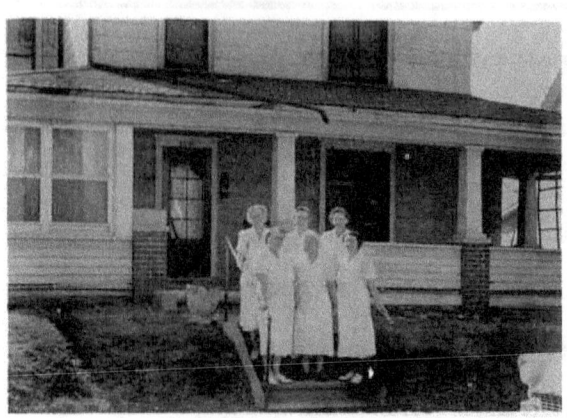

Neals Nursing Home

In business since 1951, the first Nursing Home in Trenton. Started with capacity for 8 guests have capacity for 24 at present time. We specialize in caring for the chronically ill, aged and convalesing patients, and homeless aged.

Nurse on duty 24 hours daily.

Anna C. Neal, Owner

Whitfield Plumbing

Joe Whitfield
Plumbing & Heating
Armstrong And Borg-Warner
Gas Furnaces
Phone 253

STANDING: Left to Right Harold Huff stutter, Jim Helmandollar, Cliff Waterbury, Geo. Norris, Glen Helmandollar, Claude Still, Junior Hale, Henry Stickler, Jack Briegel, Bob Browning. SEATED: Martha Maloney, Frances Briegel.

We weren't here 100 years ago but
Good Business Ideals were and -

On those same ideals of quality
and service we have built our
business.

Authorized Lincoln-Mercury
Sales and Service

HELMANDOLLAR MOTOR COMPANY

Home Of Registered Mechanics
1213 - 15 Mable Street

Trenton, Missouri   Telephone 7

Industries of The Past

Missouri Girl Cigar Factory had a thriving business for a number of years. They were once located upstairs over the present Brown Dress Shop. Clax Rentch and his brother were managers and are shown in the above photo.

Brick and Tile

A brick and tile plant with a capacity of 20, 000 bricks a day was established at the foot of Water (Main) street on the banks of the Grand river in 1906. It was known as the Trenton Brick and Tile Company with G. M. Wolz, manager. The company was strictly a local organization, the stock being held by the business men of Trenton. A huge bank of shale furnished the raw material, and the large crescent-shaped excavation west of the bridge can be seen today.

Pressed.brick, common building brick, sidewalk brick, and drain tile were manufactured, and a dozen lumber yards in north Missouri were handling Trenton brick exclusively, having found them superior to any other available material in hardness and finish. The present Baptist church was built with brick from this factory, as was the B. C. Nichols residence on Cedar, and the Harry Engle home on Chestnut. The alley extending north from the courthouse to 10th street was constructed of mud brick from this works.

The shale was ground and moulded by a dry press capable of exerting ten tons pressure to the square inch. Why did it close down? Natural gas in Kansas drove them out of business! The labor expense of fired kilns could not meet the competition.

In April, 1887, Wannamaker & Mason set up their machinery for the manufacture of their hay ricker, which was invented by Mason. The factory consisted of all the woodworking machines necessary to the manufacture, and a boiler of eighteen horsepower. The ricker would rake the hay, lift it from the ground, carry it to the stack or wagon and elevate it so that it could be placed on the stack. Later, Wannamaker opened a carriage factory, and for many years manufactured carriages, wagons, and buggies. The factory building was on West 9th just below Main St. and the building stands today about as it was in those days.

Brassfields Garage

Phone 299

13th & Harris Ave.

Trenton, Missouri

BACK ROW:(Left to Right) Lula Barry, Ethlyn Bosley, Fern Gladfelder, Elva Atkinson, Lillian Casebolt, Maggie Swinton, Belle Scott. FRONT ROW: Gertrude Johnson, Karen Clark, Winona Smith, Vern Smith.

Blue Moon Cafe

Owned And Operated By
Vern And Winona Smith

Fine Foods By Vern In Trenton For Nearly 1/2 The Centennial Year

BACK ROW: Jim Williams, Bob Ward, Fairl Clark, Tom Guile, Bob Brennenstuhl and Ray Van Meter. FRONT ROW: Mrs. J. R. Stottlemyre, Mrs. James Moore, Mrs. Hugh Brummitt, Miss Naomi Smith, Miss Rosetta Sawyer, Mrs. Adam Branham and Mrs. Eunice Wade.

The Republican-Times, Grundy County's only daily newspaper, has been published in Trenton continuously for almost a century. It got its start in 1864 as the Grand River News from Corydon, Ia. Its name was changed to Republican News in 1865.

Four years later, in 1869, Col. W. B. Rogers became the publisher. It remained under his active management until his death on Feb. 22, 1924, when his daughter, Mrs. Carrie Rogers Clark, assumed the publisher's role, which she held until her death April 5, 1946. At the time of her death, her foster son, Ray Van Meter, became the publisher and is still serving in that position.

In 1881, the Republican became a daily paper and also published a weekly. The weekly was continued until 1952 when it was discontinued.

Various names have adorned the masthead through the years but the Republican portion has been continuous since 1865.

The paper at the present time has an all-woman staff, headed by Mrs. Adam Branham as editor. Fifty women write country news and 14 boys deliver the paper in Trenton.

The Republican-Times is a member of the Associated Press News Service.

REPUBLICAN TIMES

Trenton Woolen Mills

In the spring of 1871 an industry, known as the Trenton Woolen Mills, was established in the county. This meant the end of homespun clothing. In its exuberance over the new industry the Republican fairly bubbled: We say, then, bring in your wool to the Trenton Mills--bring along your wives and daughters, also, and let them see how fast wool can be made into cloth, and we guarantee that they will go home and throw their old fashioned 'women killers' such as the spinning wheel, loom, and we may add the dye-pot, and say all honor to the enterprise that brought such a blessing for the country.'"

This woolen mill, which lasted for several years, was one of the best in northwest Missouri. It evolved out of a water mill located near what is now the south end of Main street. Messrs. D. and B. Market and Calvin Gilham were the proprietors of the mill, which did a general business in carding, spinning, reeling, and weaving. Farmers could have their own wool processed or trade it in for cloth. Cash was also paid for wool. In connection with the woolen mill, they also maintained a flouring mill.

Another flouring mill, which many of the older residents remember, was the Jennings & Fleming Bros. Mill, located towards the south end of Main street between that street and Pleasant View avenue. It was started as the Jennings Mill and later changed its name when C. F. and Henry Fleming purchased an interest in 1889. When this mill burned, C. F. Fleming assumed charge of the Charles H. Cook Mill. C. H. Cook was the father of Charles R. Cook, present head of the Cook Paint and Varnish Co.

(Continued From Page 59)
$1,000 in 1874. Since that time the following have served the Trenton school system.
1865-75--R. C. Norton; 1875-79--W. D. Dobson; 1880--John E. Vertrees; 1881--G. A. Smith; 1882-83--Minnie Hoffman; 1884-85--A. B. Cornell; 1886-87--A. B. Carroll; 1888-93--J. L. Rippetoe; 1894-98--H. E. Dubois; 1899--L. Tomlin; 1900-02--W. C. Ryan; 1903-05--Thos. B. Ford; 1906-09--Chas. A. Green; 1910--George H. Beasley (and Green); 1911-13--George H. Beasley; 1914-17--A. C. Gwinn; 1918--Eugene S. Briggs; 1919-26--Orin G. Sanford; 1927-36--W. H. McDonald; 1937--Samuel M. Rissler.

Burial Vaults & Mausoleums

Concrete Blocks-Iron Railings

Masonry Paints-Steel Windows

Pollock Mfg. Co.

800 E. 13th - Phone 1007

Plaza Gardens

In Plaza Hotel

711 Main St.

Since 1949
Sam Johnson, Street Commissioner

LEFT to RIGHT: Marie Wynne, Phyllis Hutson, Harold Buckland, Roy Simpson Jack McNabb, Richard Wynne.

ESTABLISHED IN 1902 AND HAS CONTINUOUSLY SERVED TRENTON SINCE THAT TIME.

DURING YOUR CENTENNIAL VISIT TO OUR TOWN WE INVITE YOU TO VISIT OUR STORE.

TRENTON HARDWARE

Sawmills Were Important in Those Days

MILL NEAR S. MAIN STREET BRIDGE

When the county was fairly young, many sawmills were set up within its boundaries, especially after the coming of the railroad, which caused such a demand for building material that three lumber yards could not fill the demand. In anticipation of the building boom, twenty sawmills were operating in 1870. By 1907 only four mills were left.

THANKS!

June 1st Marks Our

25th Anniversary

Entertaining This Community

-We Appreciate Your Patronage-

Plaza Theatre   Grand-Vu Drive-In

Our Business is your Pleasure

W.O. and Bill Lenhart

Layne Glass & Mirror Service

Plate Glass-Window Glass-Mirrors
Show Case Glass and Furniture Tops
Carrara For Bathrooms and Kitchens
1111 Normal St-Phone 355
Trenton, Missouri

Eat Moore's Lunch

"Eat at Eat Moore's"

26 Years at Same Location

RADIO STATION **KTTN** DIAL 1600

Seated, left to right:

LYNN BRADLEY, Chief Engineer, is "on the air" in the late morning and late afternoon. He and Mrs. Bradley (Jerry) have two children, Lynnette and Joe.

RICK McHARGUE, Program Director, has been with the station since May of '55. He and Phyllis Dolan were married June 1 of this year. He's "on the air" in the early morning, noon, and early afternoon.

Standing, left to right:

BOB DENNIS, Salesman, has one pace .... that's fast, whether it's selling advertising or giving the sports round-up in the evening.

DOROTHY DENNIS, Receptionist, is one of the busiest members of the staff with her multitude of duties. She and Bob have three children, Mike, Evelyn & Steve.

GIB KEITH, News Director, is going day and night in order to be sure he keeps K T T N listeners up to the minute on the latest news developments. He and Mrs. Keith (Dolores) have two children, Pat and Denise.

HENRY CHRISTOWSKI, Announcer, is the newest member of the K T T N staff. His chief duty is announcing, but, like everyone else on the staff, has a variety of work.

ZORA BELLE HUNDLEY, She's given up her position as receptionist in order to be able to devote more time to teaching music. However, she has a regular 15-minute program at 6:00 P.M. each Friday. She and Ed have one child, Douglas.

ED HUNDLEY, Station Manager, helped put K T T N on the air April 17, 1955. He's "on the air" with regular programs throughout the day, but spends most of his time with other phases of the broadcast business.

Drum Corps Were Popular Before The Turn of The Century

LEFT TO RIGHT: Claude Range, Harry Burrell, Charles Collier, Lute Carter, Hugh Smith, Charles Dawes, Wes. Fortney, Rufus Brown, Willie Wisdom, Dave McClain and Fred Burrill.

Farmers Mutual Insurance Co. of Grundy County

Established February 16, 1895

C. S. Mack, President

Roy Fox, Treasurer

Loren Drummond, Secretary

LEFT TO RIGHT: Mrs. Marilyn Dennis, Abstractor; Herbert S. Brown, Owner; Miss Ozella Carson, Abstractor; Mrs. Vivian C. Fisher, Manager and Abstractor.

Trenton's Newest and Best

Abstract Company

THE BEST ABSTRACT AND TITLE COMPANY
901 1/2 Main (Over Trenton Hardware), Trenton, Missouri

This Company was established in May 1956, by Herbert S. Brown, Trenton Attorney. It has complete abstract indexes to all land in Grundy County, including all town lots in each town in Grundy County.

FOR COMPLETE TITLE SERVICES
ABSTRACTS OF TITLE - ESCROWS - TITLE INSURANCE
If You Want The Best - See

Another Popular Early Day Drum Corps

L. R. Bert Burrill, Bob Walker, Sid Reed, Chas. Ballinger, Jim Collier, Bill Noah, Roy Drummond, John Dippel, Fred.Burrill, and Claude Coon.

Millard W. Ellis
New York
Life Insurance

One Policy Covering Whole Family
One Low Premium
Two New Hospital & Surgical
Expense Plans Guaranteed
Renewable For Life

Ellis
Insurance Agency
–All kinds of
Insurance

Juanita J. Ellis

915-1/2 Main Street
Phone: Office 30; Res. 1002

The Personnel of STEIN'S: Francis Mosier, Bill Estes, Mrs. Frank Carter and Owner, Nathan Stein.

In the Spring of 1869, Henry Stein came to Trenton and established a store dealing in men and ladies' clothing, dry goods and groceries. This store was located in the block near to the present location of The Nisbeth Chevrolet Company and the merchandise for the business was transported overland from Brunswick and other river ports by wagon trains.

As the town grew and moved northward, Henry Stein moved his store to a building where the Trenton Hardware Company now is and with the exception of a few years in which he engaged in the Manufacturing Business in Chicago, he continued in the retail business in Trenton in association with his sons there and later at the present location until the time of his death September 10, 1909.

Two of his sons meanwhile had left Trenton and established their own stores, namely, Maurice at Chillicothe, Missouri and Gus at Carrollton, Missouri. After the death of their Father the four sons associated with him continued the business, changing the store name from H. Stein and Sons to H. Stein' Sons. The grocery stock had several years previously been closed out and they continued with men and boys' clothing, shoes, ladies' ready-to-wear and dry goods.

In 1929 they decided to close out the Ladies' Department and moved the men's wear into the room it now occupies. At which time the north room was remodelled and divided into the three rooms it now comprises. This set-up was continued until 1938 when due to deaths of two of the brothers, Nate and Ed and the desire of the two remaining brothers, Ott and Abe, to retire they sold the store to their nephew, Nathan David Stein, who had been connected with the store since 1929.

Nathan David Stein, the present owner, took possession of the store on February 1, 1938 and changed the name to STEIN'S under which it has continued to operate carrying a complete line of men's clothing, furnishings and ladies' lingerie and hosiery.

The present owner, the son of Gus Stein, came to Trenton, March 22, 1928, from Carrollton, Missouri. Although he had grown up in the clothing business he had graduated from the St. Louis College of Pharmacy and was pursuing his profession of Registered Pharmacist prior to his coming to Trenton.

1869   STEIN'S   1957

CHAUTAUQUAS, The Big Social and

Just at the beginning of the twentieth century there spread over the United States a movement known as the "chautauqua." The movement had its inception in a large camp meeting held at Lake Chautauqua, New York; programs included lectures by well-known professional and literary men The success of the plan prompted many smaller communities, including Trenton in 1906, to organize associations and try out this mass idea of popular education. For many years, the idea proved very successful andfairly remunerative.

It was too good an idea, as was discovered, for commercial interests began to establish their chain system of chautauquas and tied up their lecturers in such contracts that independent chautauquas, such as Trenton's had to fight for their existence. The talent became mediocre in many instances, and this with the advent of the World War, marked the end of the chautauqua movement in Grundy county.

In the later period of, the development, commercial chautauquas were held in Trenton, Spickard, Galt and Laredo. In one instance, twenty-two automobiles from Spickard visited Trenton and other places advertising their chautauqua. Before the development of Moberly Park, the chautauquas in Trenton were held in the fair grounds tract; afterwards they were held in the park which was admirably suited for such gatherings. It is very probable that the holding of the chautauqua in the park was the real cause of its development and improvement.

The first officers of the Trenton Chautauqua Association, organized in 1906 were: Platt Hubbell, president; Homer Hall, vice-president; W.A. Rickenbrode, secretary; Dr. W. D. Fulkerson, treasurer.

Directors were: Revs. S. J. White, Ben F. Jones, J. G. Des singer, James B. Benton, Wiley, and Wright (all ministers of Trenton churches), and Platt Hubbell, Homer Hall, N. Guy Rogers, T. Frank Fulkerson.

For many years the movement proved extremely popular; people came from far and near to attend sessions which lasted from a week to eight days. Many rented tent sites and camped throughout the week. There were morning sessions each morning. Special entertainment was provided for the children, usually Indian lore. On Sundays, there usually being two Sundays during the program, some speaker of national reputation would be heard. One of the largest attendances was on the occasion of the celebrated evangelist, Billy Sunday, who spoke to an afternoon and evening audience. When the chautauqua was at its height, it was necessary to secure a small-sized circus tent to house the crowd.

Evening programs were largely musical and in order to satisfy those who might object to Sunday entertainments--and there were many of them in that day--the Sunday musical was always referred to as "a sacred musical concert."

The chautauqua was also a social event. The entertainers and speakers were often taken into the homes and receptions and parties were given in their honor-- especially if they were young and good looking. The "chosen few" of the town were invited to mingle. During the fair week families would rent tent space and often never leave the grounds from the time the program opened on the first day until the final curtain on the last. Various organizations had their tents and groups or families would go together and erect their shelters which formed a meeting place between programs where they would gather for a sociable hour.

James A. Hulen

Interior Decorating

Refinishing - Artistic Decoration

Antiques

Educational Event in The Early 1900's

In 1914 there were over a hundred tents on the grounds. The local newspaper on June 29 of that year reported "by one o'clock there were 67 persons in line at Secretary W. D. Stepp's office to register for tent sites at the chautauqua, and by three o'clock eighty had registered."

The first program in 1906 included such well-known names as Hon. Joseph W. Folk, "Missouri's Reform Governor"; Rev. Sam P. Jones, nationally known evangelist; Hon. Joseph G. Camp; Senator Robert M. Lafollette, later governor of Wisconsin; Montraville Flowers; entertainer; Father Nugent; Dr. W.J. Llahmon of the Missouri Bible College; Toyokichi Iyengaga of Japan; Nat Bingham; Major William Warner; and Hon. Herbert S. Hadley, later governor of Missouri.

RELAXING AT THE CHAUTAUQUA
LEFT to RIGHT: Clax Rentch, Henry Rentch, Unknown, Lila Engle, Kitty Fleming. BACK ROW: Unknown, Unknown, Mr. and Mrs. Harry Engle, Bain Fleming. STANDING: Veva Rentch, Mrs. Mike Sherwood, Clax Rentch's son.

Good Things To Eat

Free Delivery

McCarty Market

A G Food Store

DARYL BROWNING & HOMER BROWNING

Homer Browning & Son

M-M Farm Equipment
Sales & Service
Office 1300 - Res. 691
Box 501
Trenton, Mo.

PERRY HOUSE (Left)　　　　SHANKLIN-AUSTIN BANK (Right)

Street Cars

Yes, Trenton had a street car system--in fact, two systems; one was actually in operation and the other never existed except for a franchise. On October 2, 1891, a franchise was granted to N.A. Winters and company, organized and financed by Nathaniel Shanklin, C. H. Cook, George Gilmore and Capt. N. A. Winters, for a horsecar line. Within two months, the track was laid and the first street car moved away from the Rock Island station. Capt. Winters had charge of laying the car track and the ties were sold to the company by H. J. Hughes, later president of the Hughes Land and Loan company. The line was routed from the Rock Island station up what is now Tinsman avenue. There was a switch at Mabel street, one line going north on Mabel to 17th, east on 17th to Princeton road, and thence north to the fair grounds. The other line came through the business district to 9th and Main streets, then turned east on Ninth to Avalon college, the site of the present high school. Another spur ran to the southwest corner of the courthouse block.

George Mosier was the driver and conductor of the horsecar. On December 5, 1891, the Republican announced that the car now makes regular trips to all trains and will be run at any time for the accommodation of patrons. " The old timers tell us that there was no regular schedule of runs, but as a prototype of the famous "Toonerville Trolley," the conductor was obliging and would deliver packages, children and wait fifteen minutes at the street corner while mother finished lacing her corset. The line ceased operation in 1896.

Known For Finest Quality Flowers
& Originality Of Design
Eleanore Torrey Casteel - Owner
Lelia Burk McCracken
Leona Parkey Dockery
Helen V. Koch

Eleanore's Flowers

"For You"
919 Main - Phone 712

30 Years of Service To Trenton

Missouri Public Service Company, successor to the Trenton Gas and Electric Company, began service of electricity and gas to Trenton, in 1927, and has served customers here continuously since that time.

A "baby" in 1927, the Company has grown from a service to 70 towns, to one now serving 217 in Western Missouri.

The Company has operated as an Independent Company, with no "holding company" ties or controls since the present management purchased substantial stock in 1940 from the Middle West Utilities, which was a "holding company". Since then the Company has grown in customers served from 28,307 to 96,623.

In the last year, it has brought natural gas to Trenton, and 13 other north central Missouri communities, replacing here petroleum gas which had previously been sold.

Our congratulations to Trenton on its 100th Anniversary. It is our hope to continue to grow and prosper with Trenton, over the years to come.

MISSOURI PUBLIC SERVICE COMPANY

Coal Mining WAS ONCE A PROFITABLE INDUSTRY IN TRENTON

MINERS OF "SUNNYSIDE" MINE IN 1896

COAL MINING

A good part of Grundy county is underlaid with a sheet of coal from sixteen to eighteen inches thick, and at various times mines have been located at Spickard, Galt, and various locations around Trenton. This coal supply was neglected until 1873, when the Grundy County Coal Company was organized. The papers of that year told that "a coal company is being organized to prospect for coal. The parties who have taken hold of the enterprise mean business and will probe the bowels of the earth until they find the black diamonds, which doubtless underlie the town."

The first mine was sunk east of the Rock Island railroad shops and south of the O.K. Depot, and was mined at a profit for many years. Nat Shanklin was most active in the organization.

By 1883, the mine employed seventy-five miners, twenty of whom were boys under fourteen years of age. By 1887, the shaft was 210 feet deep, and seventy-five to 100 men were employed, working 300 days out of the year on the eighteen-inch vein. The men were paid $1.18 per ton, and 20,000 tons were produced a year at $2.10 per ton.

In 1891, the same company sank another shaft south of town near the railroad, almost directly south of the high school. It was called the "Sunnyside" mine. At 175 feet, a twenty-one-inch vein was struck, but the water flooded the mine and work had to be postponed until the pumps could be set up. These pumps worked constantly all the time the mine was working; the volume was such as to supply a city several times the size of Trenton. The first coal was taken out September 4, 1891.

When the old mine caught fire, burning the tipple to the ground, the Men escaped through the Sunnyside shaft, south of the city. This marked the close of the old mine, and in 1905, the Sunnyside mine was closed also. The water, combined with the distance of the face from the shaft, made further operation unprofitable.

The Trenton Mining Company, was organized in 1906, after the old mines had closed, buying part of their equipment, leases and coal rights. It was first intended that the miners buy shares of stock in the company by setting aside so much of their wages, but they refused to recognize this plan, and the shares were sold to the business men of Trenton. A new shaft was drilled adjacent to the north city limits directly west of the old fairgrounds.

Insurance

Tax   Service

Irene Fair

Phone 84   922 1/2 Main

Left to Right: Clinton Hamilton, R. D. Krehbiel, Mrs. Clara Dryer, Clarence Wilcox, John Harvey, Orville Septer, Gordon Proctor. Absent: Harry Irvin, Carl Stephens, Manford Arnold.

KREHBIEL'S

Established 1925

Progress Through The Years

First hatchery in Grundy County started with a capacity of 50, 000 expanding to present capacity of 150, 000 eggs. In 1932 purchased the Perry Smith Planing Mill building and in 1938 installed the cold storage plant, purchasing the house and lot to the south and constructing a separate building for the lockers, making a total of 15 0 feet frontage on Tinsman Avenue, entered the retail coal business which was sold in 1951 at that time doing a volume over 10, 000 tons per year. After selling the coal business entered the oil furnace business and at present both gas and oil equipment is being sold. With advent of R.E.A. an appliance store was established at which time the Philco franchise was secured and is still retained. In 1946 the old O. O.K.Y. was purchased, an area consisting of thirty-three acres within the city limits at which place we built our abattoir where thousands of cattle and hogs have been slaughtered and processed for our locker patrons, as well as home freezer owners within a twenty-five mile radius of Trenton.

Baby Chicks - Feeds - Farm Supplies - Cold Storage Lockers
Custom Slaughtering & Curing - Philco Appliances & TV
Oi 1 & Gas Heating Equipment

Grundy County Coal Mine,
DEPTH 228 FEET - ORGANIZED IN 1906 - CEASED OPERATION IN 1943

LEFT TO RIGHT: Noel Breitenbucher, Nilene Renfro, Eugene Renfro.

Tate Oil Company

Since 1920

Gasoline - Oils - Greases
Tires - Accessories - Batteries
Browning Shotguns

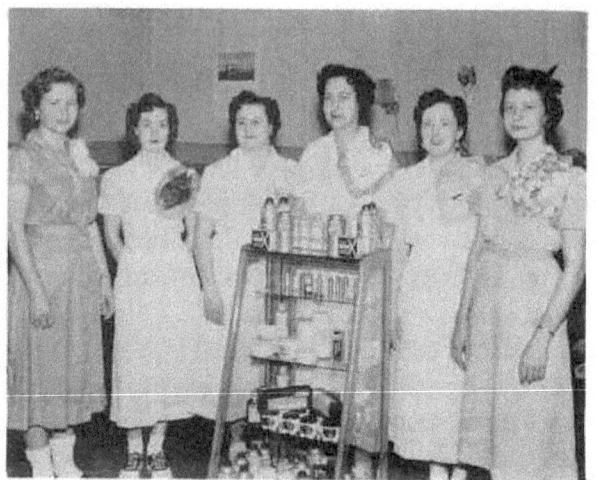

Yvette Kidd, Earlene Griffin, Dorothy Deskins, Lillie Rosson, Pauline Mayo, Pat McCaslin.

Lillie's Beauty Shop

Beauty Service at its Best

FRONT ROW: H. D. Bock, Robert Schmidt, Bill Hoskins, Jack Hunter, Denver Brown, Betty Shirley. BACK ROW: Willard Simpson, J. R. Stottlemyre, Kenneth Allen, Porter Jones, Marvin Cudney.

Where the Best Names are Found

For Quality And Service

- *INTERNATIONAL HARVESTER*
- *CADILLAC*   *OLDSMOBILE*
- *NEW HOLLAND*   *McCULLOCH SAWS*
- *RCA WHIRLPOOL*

-ESTABLISHED 1946-

BOCK TRUCK & TRACTOR CO.

Street Paving

Agitation for paving the streets, or at least for sidewalks, began in 1887, when a citizen complained in an open letter which was published by the pap'3r:

"I am compelled to say that, without exception, of all towns I was ever in, our sidewalks and streets are the very worst. True, there has been a little improvement. Brick is, to a little extent, taking the place of wood, but stone is an abomination to any people, unless dressed and trimmed to a straight edge. The great portion of our walks are still of wood, and are simply traps. The city should build walks and maintain them; charging the expense to general taxation. Cow yards and hog pens adjoin some of our walks, and smell to high heaven."

The first paving in the city of Trenton was three blocks of what is now Main street, from Ninth to Five Points and thence up what was formerly Elm to the Baptist church. This contract was awarded to W. M. Boyd and J. A. Shanklin on April 6, 1887 and they immediately put a large force of men to work grading the Water street block preparatory to macadamizing.

With the advent of the automobile the need for more extensive paving was seen, and in 1904, Water (Main) street was paved from the courthouse to Five Points at the cost of $18,000, and the next year North Elm was paved from Prospect to Bridge street at a cost to property owners of almost $8,000. The first alley to be paved was that between Main and Washington from the courthouse to 10th street. Vitrified paving brick from the Trenton Brick and Tile Company was used. In 1907, the city council ordered the paving and curbing of Chandler street, and to handle the job, a new company known as the Trenton Manufacturing and Construction Co., was organized by the property owners along Chandler street. In 1908, Prospect street from the Rock Island depot west to Norton avenue was paved. Most of this early paving was of brick, the first granitoid being used in an alley in block seven of Merrill's first addition which was described as "a new substance, cheaper than brick."

Centennial Greetings To

--- Old-Timers
--- Inbetweeners
--- Newcomers

North Missouri Lumber Co.

Life for the early settlers would have been easy if they could have had our modern services.

Serve Yourself Store

McNairs Grocery

701 3 9th

We specialize in timber clearing.

"It takes more than a bulldozer to do a complete job of timber clearing."

We have <u>complete</u> equipment:
Tree Pusher, Root Rake, and Heavy Disc.

FRED PAYNE PROJECTS →
↓

We will build you any kind of home, business plant, or building.

FRED S. PAYNE, CONSTRUCTION

Phone 1591 J-3

FRONT ROW: Seated: Left to Right: Wallace Callen, W. J. Early, Ray VanMeter, Sam Johnson, Tim Bullock, Emery Spencer. BACK ROW: Standing: Kenneth Pilcher, Jessie Hutchison, Ralph Martin, Lowell VanDyke, Art Stottlemeyer,' Glen Moore, Cleo Hobbs, Bill Foster, Quentine Spencer, Francis Stewart.

In January 1905, John Scott and Kemp Scott bought a half interest in the Newt Ratliff Grocery. In 1907, Mr. Ratliff sold his interest in the store to Gabriel Gabrielson. In July 1910, Scott Bros. bought Mr. Gabrielson's interest in the store. Then the store continued under the ownership of Scott Bros. John Scott died in 1927 and Kemp Scott continued the business as Scott Bros. till in January 1939. Scott Bros. was in business for 34 years in the same building at 1105 North Main Street.

In 1941, Kemp Scott and his sister Bell Scott opened a neighborhood Grocery and Meat Market at 815 East 7th Street which they continue to operate.

Scott Grocery

The Vigilanties

The vigilanties was organized May 5, 1933 for the purpose of assisting the local peace officers in the prevention of major crimes and giving added protection to the citizens of the community.

The organization was perfected under the supervision and suggestions of a state police officer. Total membership reached 75 members.

After a six years existence the organization ceased to be active in 1945. The organization was reorganized with a part of the original members in attendance.

Now in 1957 the organization has a membership of 21 with only three of the original group as members. Ray VanMeter, Francis Stewart, and Frank Horner.

Our principal duties now consist of assisting the police in the control of traffic, parking of cars, and general police duties at all public gatherings. However we are subject to call at all times and stand ready to give assistance at any time of need.

We operate under the same ordinances the city police, serve without pay and have the same authority as regular police officers.

Present members: President, Francis Stewart; Vice-President, Emery Spencer; Secretary, Lowell VanDyke; Tim Bullock, Wallace Callen, W. J. Early, Bill Foster, Jessie Hutchison, Frank Horner, Cleo Hobbs, Sam Johnson, Glen Moore, John Mayo, Ralph Martin, Kenneth Pilcher, Quentine Spencer, Emery Spencer, Art Stottlemyre, Wendell Stottlemyre, George Stone, Ray VanMeter, and Don Crouse.

1861 - We began abstracting with the Quill. Our records start with the County in 1841.

"IF IT'S AT THE COURTHOUSE, IT'S IN OUR OFFICE"

GRUNDY COUNTY ABSTRACT CO.

924 Main Street, Trenton, Mo.

Abstracts, Title Insurance, Photostats

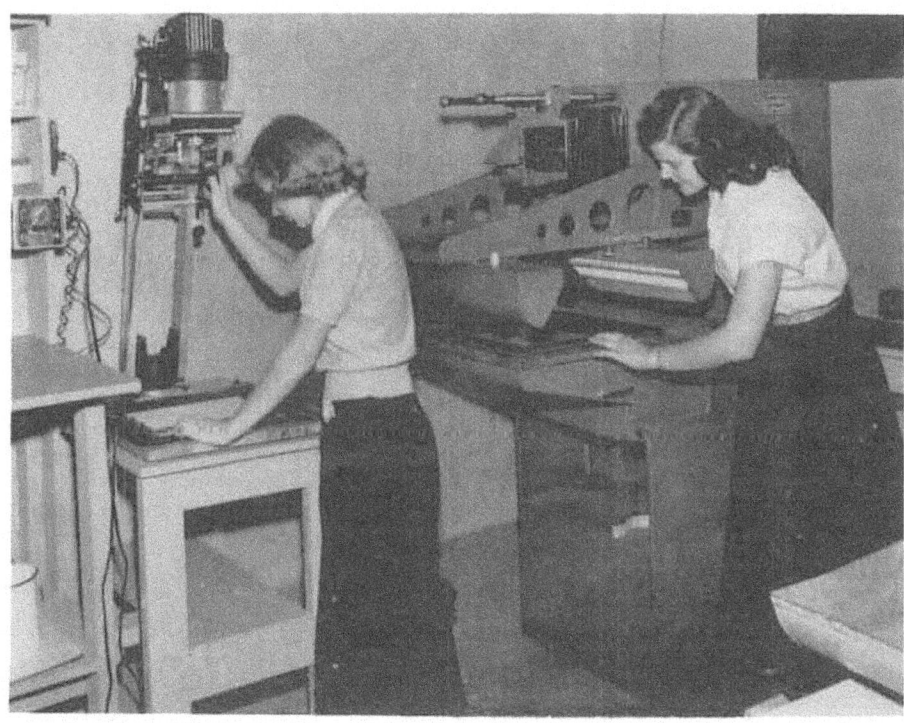

1957 - Ninety-six years of growth and progress has placed in our fireproof vaults, more than a quarter million photos of original deeds and records. Modern abstracting is by Photostat--it prevents error.

Development of the Trenton Water Plants

The first boiler put in the early water works in 1886. Moving such a huge piece of equipment was quite a job in those days, but H. H. Sawyer (in center of picture) had a rig equal to the job. Picture was taken on Main Street near Crowder Road. An interesting postscript to this story is told by Mrs. Rose Russell daughter of H. H. Sawyer, who reports that just fifty years have the installation of this first boiler, Mr. Sawyer's son T. J. Sawyer installed the next one.

Agitation for a water system began in 1885, and in April, 1886, the first water works was established just north of Moberly Park. It was completed in December at a cost of $60,000. The old reservoir is now known as Stringer's Pond and is the only remaining trace of the plant besides the ruins of a large well. The plant was operated under a twenty-year franchise by a New York company, known as the Trenton Water Company, which was organized by A. H. McCormick and C. M. Davidson of Parsons, Kansas, and W. H. Taylor of New York. Some of Trenton's most prominent businessmen were among the stockholders.

When the franchise expired in 1906, the city tried to buy the plant but the president, Herbert N. Smith of Boston, refused to sell, a board of arbitration was then appointed, consisting of C. A. Hoffman, acting for the city, and H. Wettstein for the water company. This board assessed the value of the plant at $39,000, and the city, voting a bond issue of $65,000, took over the plant July 25, 1906. The City now found itself the proud possessor of an old Triplex and a steam pump, with about six miles of various kinds of mains. After installing a new pump and repairing the machinery they agreed to build a reservoir to hold from sixty to ninety days' supply. The water could be pumped into it during the days when the rives water was clear and allowed to settle. For this purpose, a forty-acre tract, known as the old Benton farm, was purchased, and with the expenditure of $5,000 and five months' labor, a reservoir with a capacity of 65,000,000 gallons was completed in 1908. The next year it washed out during a record high water, but was replaced.

This served the purpose until new water mains were added and consequently more water used. It was then found that the reservoir would not carry over muddy water times, and September 5, 1916, the citizens voted a bond issue of $30,000 for a filtration plant. The new plant worked fine, but every silver lining has its cloud-the people liked the new water so well that the consumption increased beyond the capacity of the plant.

Up to this time the plant had paid its way and had added several thousand dollars to mains and other improvements. Then came the World War I and the prices of operation began to jump in leaps and bounds until the receipts would not pay operating expenses. At one time the city was paying $24 a ton for coal and the plant being worked to capacity. The machinery was wearing out, drainage ditches were being dug, a highway built across the bottoms, and no one could foresee the effect it would have on the water works, so the board of public works came into being, and they, in turn, hired expert engineers who formulated a water works plan.

It was decided to move the water works out of the river bottom to higher ground and avoid all chances of inundation by high water.

A bond issue of $175,000 carried, five to one, and the bonds were sold at a premium. Burns & McDonnell Engineering Co. drew up the specifications and the plant was ready for operation, February 23, 1924

THE OLD MUFF BAKERY AT 1300 MAIN ST.

MR. CHARLES MUFF, Father

THREE GENERATIONS OF BAKERS

Mr. Will Muff, Grandfather of Carl Muff was the first of 3 generations of bakers. He operated a bakery in Kansas City.

Mr. Charles Muff, father of Carl, came to Trenton in 1897 and started a bakery in back of the family home at 428 W. 15th St. In 1904, Charles Muff bought a building at 1300 Main St. and operated there several years.

In 1929, Carl Muff and his father started a bakery at 1104 Main St. In 1931, they remodeled the building at 1300 Main and moved there.

In 1949, Muff's Bakery was granted the rights to use the trade name "Holsum".

In 1954, the bakery was moved to the present location and the buildings were pruchased. This move involved a vast increase in mechanical production operation.

Muff's Bakery now operates routes covering a 50 mile radius. The plant is located on a square block allowing ample room for future expansion.

PRESENT PLANT - 200 W. 8TH ST.

GRANDSON, CARL MUFF (In White Cap) SEATED FRONT ROW CENTER.

MUFF'S HOLSUM BAKERY

200 WEST 8TH ST.   TRENTON, MO.   PHONE 346

City Gas Works Organized in 1886

In the year 1876, a proposal was made in the City of Trenton to build a gas works, the council approving the project after discussing its merits. Those interested in the plant informed the council that "while Trenton boasted of a supply of the article manufactured from wind by some of her best legal and oratorical lights, that it was a poor quality for illuminating purposes" and coal gas for lighting the streets would be preferable.

It was a good idea, but something scared the instigators, and the organization of the first gas works was left to the Trenton Gas & Electric Company organized July 16, 1886, and incorporated the winter following. The plant was valued at $20,000 and had three and one-fourth miles of mains, 130 private consumers and thirty street lamps.

The gas plant changed hands several times, finally being known as the Citizens Gas & Electric Co., which furnished coal gas for many years before it was taken over by the Missouri Public Service Company.

MOBERLY PARK

George W. Moberly, in 1886, gave to the City of Trenton a tract of twenty acres on the northwest limits of the town for a park, with the provision that this park should be known as Moberly Park, the land to be improved and forever used as a public park, It was also provided that the land 'might be sold on the vote of two-thirds of the citizens, but the proceeds should be reinvested in a similar park.

EARLY FIREFIGHTERS

The first fire company was organized in Trenton, April 2, 1873, with 38 members, and was called the "Trenton Fire King." The following officers were selected to take charge of the company and look after an increase in membership: Leve Greer, foreman; James Guerin, first assistant; George W. Smith, second assistant; Robert A. Collier, secretary; J. W. Smith, treasurer. In June, of the same year, the organization had sixty members on the roll, the limit being eighty. The reason for so many members at this time was necessitated by the "Bucket Brigade" method of firefighting.

From Left to Right: Mrs. Alfred Rowoth, Mrs. Wendell Meeker, Russell L. Whisler, Frank Reed, Mrs. Harry Huff.

Diamonds
Watches
jewelry

China
Crystal
Silver
Gifts

Mr. Reed has been in business in Trenton at the same location for 33 years. Russell Whisler bought half interest in the store in April 1955 after several years employment as watchmaker,

Reed & Whisler

1013 Main   JEWELERS   Trenton

Dependable Quality & Service Year After Year

Our Congratulations To

Trenton

1857 --- 100 Years --- 1957

We are proud to have been a part of Trenton during the past 100 years and expect to be an active part of Trenton during the next 100 years.

We are also proud that we are one of nearly 1700 Penney Stores whose aim is to give top service and first quality merchandise.

Employees Pictured - Left to Right and Front to Back: Mr. C. E. Harrison, Mgr., Mr. M. A. Pettengill, Mr. K. M. Hamilton, Mrs. Donna Wagner, Mrs. Mildred Perry, Mrs. Veta Gee, Mr. M. J. Keller, Mrs. Georgia Robertson, Mrs. Neville Young, Mrs. Grayce Fick, Mrs. Alberta Bell, Mrs. Virginia Griffin.

Theatres

The first opera house, at least of any importance, was the Hubbell Opera House, constructed in 1885 by Colonel W. W. Hubbell. For fifty years it was the leading opera house of the county, remaining in the hands of the Hubbell family all that time.

The paper of December 10, 1885, tells us that: "W. W. Hubbell contracted yesterday for a full and complete setof scenery, upon flats, consisting of fifty-six pieces. The work will be done by one of the best artists in Kansas City, and will no doubt be the finest scenery in any town the size of Trenton, in the state. The stage opening will be twenty-five feet wide and twenty-five feet deep--large enough to accommodate the most extensive traveling troupes. There will be two dressing rooms on either side of the stage in front of the latter, two proscenium boxes. A gallery twelve feet. wide and circular will be built in the rear of the hall, over the cloak rooms and box office. The seats at the back of the hall, commencing about thirty feet from the rear wall, will be elevated at an angle of about thirty degrees. Mr-Hubbell is going to furnish the house in handsome style, and when completed Hubbell's Opera House will be one of the neatest, best finished and handsomest public halls in the West--the pride of the town and a thing of beauty! " The opera house was opened February 2, 1886, with the Fireman's Ball, at which time the people of Trenton presented W. W. Hubbell with a gold-mounted opera glass as a token of their appreciation of the new opera house. The actual dedication was February 17, when probably the largest body of people to congregate under the same roof in the history of Trenton up to that time, witnessed the drama, "Ingomar. "

The capacity of the theater was one thousand people, ind it occupied the second floor of the four large business buildings on the east side of Main Street, just south of 9th. The first Vitaphone, or talking pictures appeared in this theater. It was also the scene of the trial of the Spickardsville Crusaders, and, in the early days, many of the commencement exercises were held in it, as it was the orlly building in town which could accommodate a large group of people.

The yearly social event--the Firemen's Ball--was held in the opera house, until one year Colonel Hubbell complained that it was too much trouble to take up the seats.

ARTHUR M. HYDE

One of Trenton's illustrious citizens, is remembered for his most distinguished career in public service. Although raised in Princeton he moved to Trenton in 1915, with his wife, formerly Miss Hortense Cullers and their daughter Caroline Cullers. Here he practiced law and developed an extensive automobile sales business.

He was elected Governor in 1920, and his strong individuality was reflected in morality, progress and good government. In 1929, President Hoover selected Arthur Hyde as Secretary of Agriculture and his accomplishments in the Federal branch of the government were no less outstanding than his leadership in State affairs. Mr. Hyde died on Oct. 17, 1947 and was buried in Trenton.

GENERAL ENOCH HERBERT CROWDER, 1859-1932

General Crowder the originator of the first World War draft was born in Edinburg in 1859. His early education was received at the old Grand River College, which at that time was the most prominent educational institution in the North Central Missouri. On completing the course there, young Crowder entered the United States Military Academy in Sept. 1877.

During the Spanish American War he became judge Advocate of the American Expeditionary Forces. He then served in the Philippines and did much to develop a new body of laws for that country. He became judge Advocate General of the Army in 1911, and developed the Selective Act of 1917. In June 1918 the Senate passed a bill conferring upon him the rank of Lt. General, but General Crowder himself refused the proffered rank explaining that many others had contributed to the execution of the Selective Service Act.

Harold Perry
Electric Service

In Business 12 Years

Wiring and Installation

721 Emma   Phone 615

BACK ROW: Left to right; Earl Ballew, Mgr., Robert Cooksey, Jesse Ament, Donald Whitney, Phillip Schlarb, Richard McCloud, Henry Harlow. FRONT ROW: Kenneth Buzzard, Doris Constable, Beverly Worland, Darleen Constable, and Delbert Gentry.

WE'LL BE HERE TO SERVE

YOU WHEN THE

1957 Centennial

IS A MEMORY

Grundy County Fairs

The last reorganization occurred in 1943 with the advent of the North Central Missouri Fair, which was incorporated in 1950. The old fairgrounds being no longer available, new grounds were secured with the co-operation of the city of Trenton, in the vicinity of Eastside Park. Utilizing the well built "Rock Barn" and new livestock buildings subsequently erected by the Fair Board, this new venture in fairs indicates that early failures were not in vain and that Trenton through this experience has become known throughout the state as the site of The North Central Missouri Fair. A fine dirt race track was also built just west of Eastside Park and is operated throughout the summer months by the Fair Board.

Grundy County Fairs

The vicinity of Chestnut and West Fourteenth streets was the home of Trenton's first fair. It commenced September 30, 1868, and continued three days. However, the matter of forming a fair association had been discussed many years previously, for in 1859, farmers of the county organized an association, drew up a petition to the county court and asked as a corporate name, The Grundy County Agricultural and Mechanical Society. The order of the court is a matter of record in October, 1859, and had it not been for the Civil War, which began shortly afterward, the association might have had a longer and more successful history.

Two fairs were held by this organization, both being successful beyond all expectations and forming a stepping stone for the next organization which took over its functions after the war.

The North Missouri Central Agricultural and Mechanical Association was actually formed on March 9, 1868, with the following men as directors: Edwin Ryder, Chas. Skinner, H. J. Herrick, G. W. Gibson, Josiah Barnes, G. W. Moberly, C. R. Webster, J. H. Shanklin, J. M. Leedy, Benj. Lockhart and P. H. Yakey. Capital stock was $5,000, divided into shares of ten dollars each. A tract of land, consisting of twenty-two and one-half acres was purchased and fenced with a board fence nine feet high. This was the tract north of the O.K. railroad and east of Princeton road. This association continued to hold its fairs with varying degrees of success until about 1873 when an effort was made to associate other counties in the project. The plan failed because the other counties wanted to have the seat of the fair. The "grand district" was to be composed of Livingston, Daviess, Harrison, Mercer, Sullivan, Linn, and Grundy.

A new organization was formed in 1876, taking over the name and many of the old members of the preceding organization, besides assuming the debts. For twenty-five years this organization sponsored the fair in the months of September or October of each year. The gates of the grounds were opened at 7 o'clock each morning of the fair, and the exhibition commenced at ten. A man on foot was admitted for a quarter, team and wagon another quarter, the same for a horse and buggy, and fifteen cents for a saddle horse.

11 reorganization took place in 1901, with the incorporation of The Grundy County Fair Association. It started with $5,000 capital, purchased the old fair grounds, widened and remodeled the track, making it an ideal half mile dirt track. A large amphitheater was built to be used as a grandstand, which was said to seat 5,000 people; there was also Floral Hall for exhibits, a judges' stand, and plenty of large shade trees, making an ideal place for picnics and outings, and in later years was used as the site for the annual chautauquas.

An attempt was made to reorganize the association in 1920, but it was an unsuccessful venture. The association by 1927, had an indebtedness of $7,500 and efforts were made by the county court to take over the grounds as a public park. Stockholders were asked to sign their shares over to the county; many did so, but the deal was never consummated, and shortly thereafter the grounds were taken over and auctioned off into lots. All of the buildings were removed, the grounds leveled off, and little is left today of the beautiful tract which once housed and held the largest crowds ever assembled in Grundy county.

Centennial Greetings From
The Board of the North Central Missouri Fair

GUY RATLIFF
President 1950

CLELL CARPENTER
President 1951

OTHO NISBETH
President 1952

OWEN McVAY
President 1953

ALFRED WITTEN
President 1954

ELMER POSEY
President 1955

S. L. BROWN
President 1956

FLOYD PEW
President 1957

FRANCIS KARR
Vice-President 1957

Bicycle Races Were Featured at the Early Fairs

Left to right: 1st Bicycle, unknown; 2nd, Ben McGuire on cycle, 3rd, W. D. Stepp on cycle; 4th, Harry Does on cycle with Wm. Gipson as starter.

The original hotel that was built in 1885. The hotel that was built by Chas. Sears in 1930 as it is at present. Owners and operators, Mr. and Mrs. Ed. Logsdon.

Hotel Plaza

GRUNDY ELECTRIC COOPERATIVE

Light - Heat - Power

Supplying Electric Power And Service To 52 00 Rural Consumers

Over 2000 Miles Of Rural Lines In Grundy, Harrison, Mercer, And

Sullivan Counties, Missouri,

And Wayne County, Iowa

AN INTERESTING EVENT TOOK PLACE DURING THE **1903 Fair**

Mr. & Mrs. Fred Thomas, parents of Mrs. James D. Holcomb, were married in front of the grandstand. Tom Witten and C. Berry are on the driver's seat. Note: This must have been the formula for a long and successful married life. Mr. & Mrs. Thomas are happily married and now live in Trenton.

Mr. & Mrs. W. D. Johns

We Opened Our Dairy Queen In Trenton, June 1, 1954
We Are Young In Town, But Dairy Queen's Quality Takes Care Of The Experience

Dairy Queen

Centennial Greetings
1944   1957
We Have Always Featured Top Quality Food
Our Pledge Is To Continue To Do So

Chumbley's Grocery Store

811 Emma St. - Phone 10

BANKS ARE PEOPLE
The Trenton Trust Team

DEDICATED TO

FRONT ROW: Bettie Shaw, Lois Hann, Deva McHargue, Evelyn Russell, Judy Payne

BACK ROW: Haynes Drummond, Robert C. Brown, Willis Alexander, Curtis LaFollette, W. W. Alexander, George Constant.

Serving  You

LEFT TO RIGHT: Ray Van Meter, Haynes Drummond, Willis Alexander, M. J. Furlong, W. W. Alexander, Ed. Knudsen, T. L. Rehard, R. D. Krehbiel, (Not in Picture) A. V. Spillman.

and
The Trenton Community

Many Special Events Featured The Old Fair

NOT THE LATEST MODELS-- BUT SPEEDY IN THOSE DAYS

See Us First, Last and Always
The Best in Real Estate Service

Bob Broyles Land & Loan Co.

(Incorporated)
Realtors Since 1946

Trenton   Missouri

LEFT TO RIGHT: Russell Campbell, Mr. and Mrs. Henry Hurst. NOTE: Mr. M. Tuckwiller is not shown.

    This is the headquarters for Surge Dairy Farm Equipment for the fifteen county North Central Missouri area. The Surge line includes pail type milkers, parlor stalls, syphon pipe line system, water heaters, automatic clean-in-place systems, and systems controlled by the Surge Electrobrain.
    Mr. Hurst has been with Surge since January 1948. At first he was with George Muck. After buying Mr. Muck's interest in the business in October 1952, he moved to the present location. Marion Tuckwiller and Russell Campbell are employed to cover the area in panel trucks. Mrs. Hurst helps in the office and does the bookkeeping.

Surge Sales & Service

Phone 486   1018 E. 13th

Owned By

Henry P. Hurst

Early Post Offices

TRENTON POST OFFICE
IT TOOK SIXTY YEARS
Built In 1932

The post office history of Trenton has indeed been a turbulent one, especially in the last sixty-five years. The first residents of Trenton came in 1834, but it was six years before they succeeded in getting government mail service and a recognized post office. Before this time, Spring Hill in Livingston county and Millport in Daviess or Ray county were the nearest post offices with Lomax's Store as the general place of delivery. Any person from this vicinity who happened to be traveling through those places took it upon himself to bring all the mail for the neighborhood and leave it at Lomax's Store to be called for.

Thus Trenton's first name was Lomax's Store, and James S. Lomax, the proprietor, was the first postmaster. The first post office was established October 19, 1840 and Lomax officially installed as postmaster of Bluff Grove, which was the name given to the new community by the post office department. It kept this name a year and a half before it was changed to Trenton, February 17, 1842. Lomax was still postmaster, and continued to hold the position until October 17, 1845, when he was succeeded by George W. Moberly.

Navigation on Grand River?

More than a hundred years ago, the legislature of Missouri declared Grand river to be a navigable stream "to the northern boundary of the State"-an absurd statement to the generation of today who know Grand river only as a drainage ditch; a highly improbable statement to those who knew the river before it was straightened; but only a slight exaggeration to those who know the facts.

The year 1844 brought with it a flood-they came regularly every seven years-and in that year William Perry built two flatboats, loaded them with wheat at Trenton and took them to St. Louis. Seven years passed and another inundation came in 1851. All the bottom lands were under water and mail service was held up for six weeks, but the people reasoned that some good must come of the high water and agitation began to make the river navigable at least to Trenton. A letter to the editor of the Western Pioneer reveals the hope of the times.

LaPetite Beauty Shop

We'll be here to serve you after the 1957 Centennial is a memory.

DON ATKINSON

Hand Tooled Belts - Ladies' Hand Bags
Billfolds Made To Order

Atkinson Boot Shop

TRENTON, MISSOURI

Makers of Fine Handmade (Cowboy) Boots

DON ATKINSON
Next Door to
Veach Saddlery
23rd & Princeton Road

GUARANTEED TO FIT AND PLEASE.
Ask or Write for Catalog.

"Our Boot Customers Are World-Wide"

LEFT to RIGHT: Everet Frey, Wayne Eaton, Bernadine French, Willard Skinner, Ashley Thomas, E. M. Gardner, C. W. Skinner. FRONT ROW. Robert E. Skinner,

Founded 35 years ago by E. M. Gardner and C. W. Skinner, this store--since 1922--has grown with Trenton.

Primarily a battery and automotive electric shop, this business was started in the old Ward mill building, where the A & P store now stands. In 1925, they built a 50 x 50 building on Monroe street, where the older part of the shop is now, and in 1949 built the front part of the building facing East 9th street.

Handling the first radios that came out in 1923 and 1924, the business began to grow. They have been a FRIGIDAIRE dealer for 24 years.

TODAY with one of the largest and most modern showrooms in north Missouri, a complete line of electrical appliances are handled.

COME in the next time you are in town---you will be welcomed.

GARDNER & SKINNER ELECTRIC CO.

213 EAST NINTH   PHONE 400

Building the New Bridge East of Trenton

CENTENNIAL GREETINGS

From

Trenton's Chiropractors

The above Doctors of Chiropractic, members of the world's largest drugless healing profession are:

Left Sitting, Dr. F. R. Oberlag; Right Siting, Dr. C. M. Klinginsmith; Left Standing, Dr. R. W. Browning; Right Standing, Dr. L. J. Robinson

THROUGH THE YEARS

THE BEST POSSIBLE TELEPHONE SERVICE

AT THE LEAST POSSIBLE COST

CONSISTANT WITH FINANCIAL SAFETY

SOUTHWESTERN BELL TELEPHONE CO.

Leading Citizens of Trenton

AT THE TURN OF THE CENTURY

TOP ROW: Left to Right; Unknown, T. N. Witten, "Mon" Thomas. MIDDLE ROW: Frank Hoffman, Ed. Patterson, "Buck" Mason. FRONT ROW Ott Stein, W. H. Crooks.

Gas Furnaces

Gas Conversion Burners

Holland Furnace Co.

C. W. Tener, Manager

---

100 Good Wishes From

Hopewell Boyce Agency

Ins. Office - 512 Linn St.

1/4 The Age Of Trenton

Centennial Greetings

Modern Today in Cosmetology

and Hairdressing.

Lucille Mistler Beauty Shop

Evelyn Bosley Beauty Shop

Mildred, Bones, Sam Crutcher, Tommy Lame, Lawrence Ricketts

CENTENNIAL GREETINGS FROM "BONES" AND THE GANG

LIONBERGER AUTO PARTS

Early Grocery Stores BOUGHT THEIR MERCHANDISE IN BULK

Here in Fitterer and Hoffman's Grocery there were no TV and radio advertised delicacies daintily wrapped in cellophane. All items were taken from a box or barrel and weighed on the grocery scale. The store was later known as Fitterer and Crooks and was destroyed in a disastrous fire in the 90's. It was located where the second door of Montgomery Ward's is now. The Farmers Store was on the left and C. A. Conrad store on the north.

Atkinson-Windle Co.

Ready-Mixed Concrete
Hot & Cold Mix Asphalt
Reinforcing Steel-Concrete Blocks

Phone 256

Trenton, Mo.

Bob Wildman

Your
Lennox Heating
and
Air Conditioning Dealer

2001 East 9th

LEFT to RIGHT: Marge Achenbach, Connie Sue Long, Edward Gott, John Kennedy, Richard Allnutt, Dwight Miller, Frank Achenbach.

Trenton, We Salute You, On Your 100th Year, Our Tenth of A Century Here Has Been Successful and Happy, and We Are Grateful To You, Our Many Good Friends and Valued Customers.

HOME GAS & APPLIANCE

1117 Main

"The Best in Gas Appliance & Gas Appliance Service"

Group of Local Businessmen and Rock Island Officials AT THE RIVERSIDE COUNTRY CLUB IN ABOUT 1916

Trenton Band 1904

TOP ROW: Ed Walker, L. J. Matejka, Geo. T. Dull, Bain Fleming, Rufus Daniels. SECOND ROW: Elmer Speer, Henry Rensch, Wm. Thomas, James Baker, Fred Drummonds. FRONT ROW: Claude Maggard, Ed Baker, Claude McCracken.

THE EBBE CONSTRUCTION CO.

C. C. EBBE

INCORPORATED IN 1929

C. C. Ebbe started contracting in Trenton in 1919. During his lifetime the Company did some bridge and highway work and built a number of prominent buildings in Trenton---among them Norton School, the High School, Central Farm Products, the Bean Plant, the Municipal Electric Plant, Helmandollar Motor Co. and the Municipal Swimming Pool.

In 1947 Earl Ebbe joined his father in the Company, and since that time the Company has built an addition to the Municipal Electric Plant, Nisbeth's Garage, the Presbyterian Church, Ebbe's Office, St'd Oil Bulk Station, Bock's St'd Station, Phillips Oil Station, and Colonial Oil Station. Contracts for power plants have been fulfilled in Marshall, Anthony, Kansas, Blackwell, Oklahoma; and Clarksdale, Mississippi; a swimming pool in Carrolton, and a school at Bosworth, Missouri. Several Trenton homes have been built by the Ebbe's and the Company has done innumerable remodeling and repair jobs.

E. E. EBBE

PRESBYTERIAN CHURCH

EBBE'S OFFICE - 914 WASHINGTON

MUNICIPAL UTILITIES

JACKSON'S "PHILLIPS" STATION

WORKMEN

NISBETH CHEVROLET COMPANY

CENTRAL FARM PRODUCTS

A Good Four Horsepower Outfit DID THE ROAD GRADING AROUND TRENTON IN MARCH 1913.

Left: R. S. Hatfield   Right: Will Leahue

Left to Right: Dale Clark, Ray Thomas, Cecil Ellis, Seigle Moore and Robert Lovell

Transport & Tank Wagon Deliveries
Gasoline & Fuel Oils

Phone 444   **Hy Power Oil Co.**   1501 Lulu

LEFT to RIGHT: Wally Callen, Norman Meighen, Lloyd Gannon

FRONT ROW: Nettie Hobbs, Thelma Clark, Fannie Ewing, Cuma Duke, Ruth Hoskins, Irene Evans, Marie Culp, "Blondie" Callen. BACK ROW: Dora McLaughlin, Cleo Stanturf, Verna Norris, Phyllis Elliott, Pearl Shira, Norman Meighen, Lloyd Gannon, Wally Callen.

We Offer the Finest in Dining Facilities
and Modern Car Servicing

HY POWER CAFE & OIL CO.

Hyway 6.5 North

Can You Remember WHEN AUTOMOBILES WERE REPAIRED IN THE LOCAL BLACKSMITH SHOPS?

Geo. Clinkenbeard's Blacksmith Shop In 1915 At 13th And Lulu Sts.

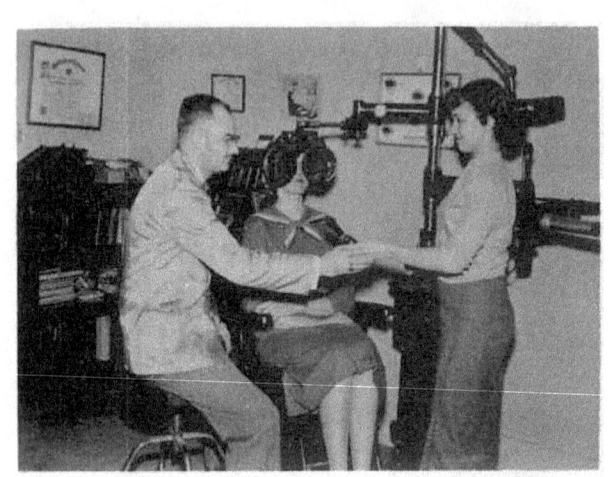

Dr. J. D. Holcomb,

Optometrist

First Choice With Farmers
For 40 Years

Federal Land Bank Loans

Water and electric plant operators: Left to Right L. D. Kerrpton, Manager; Ike Ralston, Homer Holloway, Raymond Croy, Cleo Gass, Joe McClure, Pat Wallace, Donald Shipley, and Cort Grubb.

Office and Service employees: Front: Left to Right: Shirley Clodfelter, Lillian Barnes, Mabel Drummond, Tommie Weston. Center: Left to Right: Lloyd Kerns, L. Kempton, Manager; Richard Haney, Clyde Stringer, Donald Brennenstuhl, Okie Moss. Back Row: Left to Right: Woodie Jones, Oakley Stottlemyre, Eldon Denison, Robert Jones. Employees not shown: William Hoffman, Nelson Washburn.

An election called for April 4, 1933, to vote $250,000 in bonds for a plant, failed by a vote of 1563 to 1630. Another election was called November 14, 1933, and this time the bonds carried by a vote of 1998 to 861.

Burns & McDonnell were employed as consulting engineers to secure, prepare, and compile all engineering data, and also information in reference to an application to the Federal Emergency Administration of Public Works for a loan of approximately $250,000, and, December 5, 1934, an ordinance passed approving a loan and grant agreement with the government, wherein the government would loan the city an amount not in excess of $315,000 for the light plant. On March 4, 1935, $242,000 in bonds were purchased by the Chase National Bank of New York, and on the last day of August, of the same year, the loan and grant agreement between the city and the United States was terminated. Note: These bonds are being completely paid in this centennial year.

Three different contracts were awarded; one for the equipment, one for the plant, and one for the distribution system. The Fairbanks, Morse, and Company was awarded the contract for installing the power plant equipment, September 8, 1936, for $119,543. The equipment included three Diesel engine driven generator units and all auxiliary equipment. Mattison, Wallack and Co. were awarded the contract for the distribution system, on the same day, for $96,935. The plant building contract was awarded to the Ebbe Construction Company, December 3, for $10,439. October 25 of the following year, a contract was awarded to the Sangama Electric Co. for the installation of meters.

By November 1, 1937, the plant was in operation, supplying power to the street lights, and a week later to the houses and stores.

In 1945 another 980 kilowatt Diesel engine was purchased from Fairbanks Morse and paid for in cash out of plant earnings.

In 1948 a fifth engine of 1130 kilowatts was purchased from Fairbanks Morse, being paid for by cash and revenue bonds.

The distribution system has been tripled since the original installations.

The present manager of the Trenton Municipal Utilities is Lester D. Kempton, and the Board of Public Works are: Ray V. Denslow, chairman, E. Knudsen, Dr. C. H. Cullers and C. W. Skinner.

TRENTON MUNICIPAL UTILITIES

The First Sewing Machine Store

Mr. A. B. Crooks (with cap) first brought sewing machines to Grundy County to sell.

Hazel Van Fleet, owner; Thressa Lovell, Maxine Hill, Dale Garrison, Nancy Johnson, Chloe Wilford.

FOR THE BEST FOOD IN TOWN

Van's Chat & Chew

Hudson Radio & Television Service

We Service Any Make or Model
We Specialize in Auto Radios

Pickup and Delivery-Phone 493

Trenton, Missouri

CENTENNIAL GREETINGS
From the Lawyers of Trenton

BACK ROW: Left to Right; Russell N. Pickett, Charles J. Hoover, Phil Hauck. FRONT ROW: Charles A. Miller, Harry J. Fair, L. A. Warden, Herbert S. Brown. Thomas J. Layson. INSET LEFT: Eugene E. Andereck. INSET RIGHT: Leroy R. Miller.

Geo. H. Hubbell

Birdseye View of Trenton
FROM THE CLOCK TOWER ON CENTRAL SCHOOL IN THE NINETIES

A & A Termite Control

18 Years in This Service

10 Years in Trenton

Reliable & Dependable

Phone 917

"See Doss BEFORE a Loss"
Howard Doss - Mary Doss

Low Rates   Dependable Service

Doss Insurance Agency

1948   1957

STANDARD OIL COMPANY

Serving Trenton Community For Three Quarters Century
From Coal Oil and Axle Grease To
Todays Modern Fuels & Lubricants
Howard Laffoon Standard Oil Agent
John Bailey, Sales Agent - Roy Holloway, Driver

Jim Pennell
Pennells Standard Service
Highway 65 Cutoff - Ph. 197

Woody Oyler
Oyler Standard Service
212 East Ninth - Ph. 539

Who Remembers When the Floor Collapsed
DURING THE REMODELING OF THE TRENTON NATIONAL BANK IN 1910

The Biggs Hatcheries

Leslie Self, Manager
Home of Biggs Better Bred Baby Chicks- U. S. Pullorum Typhoid Clean
Phone 15

BLAIR CERTIFIED FEED   Trenton, Missouri   GENERAL MILLS LARRO FEEDS

FRONT ROW: Norma Oswalt, Shirley Lovell, Joan Goodman, Patsy Trump, Elna Oswalt, Pauline Lovell. BACK ROW: Opal Hutchens, Della Reid, Anna McKay, Winona Stottlemyre, Zelda Newman, Charlene Metcalf, Lila Dickey, S. A. Dickey.

S. H. Kress & Co. first opened in Trenton on Sept. 1, 1910 and later was remodeled, enlarged and reopened on Oct. 27, 1939. As in the past years, we wish to give the best possible service that can be given to our customers.

A Group of Prominent Trenton Men
PICTURED AT MT. VERNON AUG. 9, 1890
Note: It is Possible That They Were in Washington D. C. to Attend a G. A. R. Meeting as Several are Carrying Civil War Hats.

LEFT to RIGHT: Amos Bottsford, M. Wetzler, L. Gass, T.A. Murphy, Unknown, Mr. Irving, W.H. McGrath, W. H. Shanklin.

Paul Henderson, Paul McArtor Jr. Harold Hughes, Donald Levienx, Carl Wiebe.

CONGRATULATIONS TO

TRENTON ON ITS

100TH YEAR.

WE WILL CONTINUE TO

SPECIALIZE IN TIRE SERVICE.

A TIRE FOR EVERY NEED

AND PURPOSE.

Good Year Service Store

TRENTON, MISSOURI

BACK ROW: Chas. Holmes, Stanley Covey, James Briegel, Raymond Scott. FRONT ROW: Eldon Spencer, Elmer McLaughlin, Glen Gates. NOT PRESENT: Wendell Heckman, Jerry Ward.

HOLMES TRACTOR PARTS & SERVICE

A Satisfied Customer Is Our First Consideration

Dance Committee OF THE BROTHERHOOD OF LOCOMOTIVE FIREMEN IN 1895 AT THE HUBBLE OPERA HOUSE.

LEFT TO RIGHT: Unknown, Tom McDonald, Unknown, Joe Proffitt, C. D. McCallum, A. R. Canady, Unknown, Marty McDonald, C. R. Custard, John Kackley.

Modern Motel

Package Store

The

Gables

North Missouri's
Leading Supper Club
Open 5 PM To 1:30 AM
We Specialize In
Steaks - Chicken
Sea Foods
Dancing After 9:30 PM

Hy. 6S North - Phone 598

The above picture of the interior of the Bakyr's Store and its employees, reading left to right: Mrs. Dwight Walker, Mrs. Charles Woods, Mrs. John Kessler, C. E. Hollingsworth, Mgr., Mrs. Clarence Hollingsworth, Kenneth Brown Jr. and John Hollingsworth.

The Bakyr's Department Store is located at 1000 Main Street in one of Trenton's newer buildings, which was built especially for them in 1951, after a fire had completely demolished one of Trenton's old town sites, a building occupied for years by the H. C. Steer and Sons Co., and later housed The Farmers Exchange Bank. The second floor housed the Moose, and Eagle Lodges, where many of the city's dances and festivities were held. Bakyr's Department Store is located on one of Trenton's historical land sites, better known as Five Points. There are many legends as to why this location was called Five Points, but today it is used by the community as a central location spot for the city.

The Bakyr Department Store

J. M. BAKYR
President and Founder of The J. M. Bakyr Mercantile Co.

Mr. Bakyr has been a long time resident of the state of Missouri, beginning his career as a merchant in Hickory Creek. Later in 1930 Mr. Bakyr opened The Bakyr Department Store at Stansberry, Mo. Followed by stores located at Chillicothe, Albany, and Maryville, Missouri, Clarinda, Iowa, and finally Trenton, Mo. Mr. Bakyr is exceptionally proud of the high quality merchandise carried in all of his stores, and the standard on which they are run. His motto, ("Where Good Quality Is Never Expensive") is indeed an omen as to how he feels toward the Trenton community.

Harness Shops Were Important BEFORE THE COMING OF THE AUTOMOBILE

W. C. Dye's Harness Shop offered a great variety of equipment. Horse collars, blankets, and harness are items the younger generation has had no opportunity to see.

The Nielsen Oil Company

Operated by Galen Nielsen with the assistance of Olin Meek, Floyd Trump, Monroe Harris and Dale Leeper.

Established business September, 1937.

Handle Texaco Products, Firestone Tires, Autolite Batteries, Johnson Outboard Motors and Aluma Craft Boats and a complete line of fishing and hunting equipment.

LEFT TO RIGHT: Harley Owens, E. L. Griffith, Thornton Cox, Ernest Burley, Lena Mapel, Shannon Evans, Patsy Briscoe, Earnest Loder, Charles Woods, Richard Holloway, J. H. Cook, Mayor and forma manager, C. P. Carroll, Bill Erwin. NOT PICTURED: Sam Sloggy, A. W. Nance, Charles Perry, L. K. Potter, R. H. Smith, Wayne Suddith, F. B. Estes, several other seasonal employees.

The history of Swift & Company in Trenton extends over a period of 58 years during which operations have been carried on in two sets of buildings. The original plant, a frame structure, that was sold to Swift & Company in 1899 three years after it was built was completely destroyed by fire in 1912. A new building was built on the same site and in this plant we have operated 'the business since that time. The creamery was started in the spring of 1914.

Swift & Company entered the dairy and poultry business in 1899 when the E. C. Lightner plant, established three years previously by Mr. Lightner, was bought. This was one of the first dairy and poultry plants in the Swift plant organization. The company had entered the poultry business only the year before, had found that what was needed was plants near the source of supply, and had begun to buy or lease poultry dressing plants in the most productive areas of the midwest.

Swift bought Mr. Lightner's plant on the condition he would manage the business. This he agreed to do, and he was with the company for the next 12 years. The managers of the plant since its original purchase have been as follows:

E. C. Lightner	1899 to 1911
Drexel Lightner	1911 to 1912
Arthur Anderson	1912 to 1914
C. T. Nichols	1914 to 1915
J. H. Cook	1915 to 1928
R. F. Gantt	1928 to 1936
E. Loudenburg	1936 to 1937
R. F. Gantt	1937 to 1938
J. H. Cook	1938 to 1951
E. W. Patterson	1951 to 1957
C. P. Carroll	1957 to ----

We are proud of the long service record of the present employees. J. H. Cook, present Mayor of Trenton, retired manager, had a service record of 42 years when retired. Other long service records include:

E. Loder	- 42 years	R. Smith	- 23 years
Lena Mapel	- 32 years	E. Burley	- 22 years
C. P. Carroll	- 31 years	W. S. Erwin	- 17 years
E. L. Griffith	- 33 years	S. Sloggy	- 19 years
H. Owens	- 29 years	E. Potts	- 17 years
F. B. Estes	- 29 years	R. Holloway	- 15 years
H. Murrell	- 27 years	A. W. Nance	- 15 years
T. Cox	- 25 years		

Swift & Company

DAIRY & POULTRY PLANT
1426 Lulu Street
Trenton, Missouri
Creamery - Poultry - Eggs - Hatchery, Both Chicks and BBB Nicholas Turkey Poults - Feed
Phone - Plant - 383   Phone - Hatchery - 22

In The "Good Old Days" Parades BROUGHT OUT SOME VERY FANCY VEHICLES. THIS PRIZE WINNER IS LINED UP ON MAIN STREET NEAR THE LIBRARY.

STANDING: Right to Left Jesse Pringle, Conrad (Unknown), Helen Grove McVay, Lela Schooley Fulkerson, Lucy Crooks, Eithel Caldwell.

Dr. Leslie Green

Serving Trenton

12 Years

HUFFSTUTTER

Used Cars

My Many Years In The Automobile Business Insures The Best Quality In Used Automobiles.

Frank Huffstutter

Jacksons "66" Service Station

Located at 1843 E. 9th, opened Oct. 1955, serving Trenton and the surrounding community with its completely modern facilities. Under its present management since that time.

Remember Jackson's Phillips "66" Service is where "Courtesy Dwells and Service Excels".

Phone 534   Paul and Don Jackson

Eads Oil Company

The business was started by Tom Eads in 1933 who retired in 1955. It is now operated by his son, Donald Eads and daughter, Edna Lager, assisted by Tommy Ray Eads and Bob Lager. Bob is serving in the U. S. Air Force at the present time and will be active in the business when he returns home. Left to right: Don Eads, Bob Lager, Edna Lager, Tom Eads, Dan Curtis, Homer Murphy and Boyd Yerby. In front: Tommy Eads.

Street Improvement in 1893

North Water St. (now Tinsman Ave.) had quite a ceremony when the project started. Left of Picture (left to right): Jet Ward, Young Glen Drinkard with his father Bill Drinkard, Orville Shanklin. Center, Joseph Scott, street commissioner; on right (right to left): Sam Love, Gus Barth, Henry Wettstein, Dave Norton.

TUNE IN — the National Farm and Home Hour, NBC, Saturday

ALLIS-CHALMERS
SALES AND SERVICE

Medcalf Implement Co.
1938 E. 9th

Names under picture - Merle Ebbe, Mona Turner, Deborah Pease, Emma Francis.

Styles Reflect The Times
You'll Find Only The Latest When
You Shop At

The Emily Shop

The Only "Old Fashioned" Idea at Boehner's is Our

Low Prices Every Day of The Week

We are Proud of Our New Store in This Old Town, We Are Trenton's
Only Home Owned Super Market - Growing With Trenton

Boehner's I. G. A. Super Market

2001 East 9th Street   Trenton, Missouri

In 1904 This Means of Transportation Served Very Well

TAKEN IN FRONT OF THEM. E. CHURCH

MFA Dairy Breeders of the Missouri Farmers Association is happy to join in congratulating the city of Trenton on 100 years of progress. We believe that Trenton and Grundy County are destined to have many more years of success.

We feel that our service in artificial insemination has and will continue to contribute materially to the standard of living of farmers in Grundy County.

Our representative in Grundy County is Cloy Gass.

MFA Dairy Breeders

Springfield, Mo.

J. Burdman Auto Parts, Inc.

Northern Missouri's Largest

Automotive Distributor

Serving Northern Missouri For 33 Years

Trenton Mo. For 19 Years

The Personnel of the local Ward Store as pictured above are: BACK ROW: Left to Right: Paul Duke, Don Johnson, Homer Burress, Billy Grimes, Mansel Ellis, Edna Hobbs, Lenys Wallace, Lionel Dean, Ralph Walsh, Clyde Griffin, Herschel McCullough, Paul Cash, Bill Martin, Lowry Crawford. MIDDLE ROW: Ethel Tennant, Alice Septer, Marjorie Powers, Allene Maloney, Jean Hughes, Clara McCollum, Alma Powell. FRONT ROW: Edna Rumbley, Arnetta Croy, Shirly Overton, Frances Rentfro, Mary Carr. Other employees not pictured are: Andy Williams, Virgil Thomas, John Harvey, Evelyn Ferguson, Leonard Weaver, Geo. Lemley,- Gil Griffin, jean Geyer, Ruby Lindsay, Irene Robertson.

The Montgomery Ward Store

The Montgomery Ward Store has been located in Trenton since 1936 in the Old Farmers Store building at 1 0th and Main Streets.

Montgomery Ward will be celebrating its centennial in a few years and is the oldest and first company to publish a catalog and sell by mail. The first catalog was a 2 page leaflet and has now- grown to hundreds of pages offering 130,000 items.

Old Central School in 1908

Centennial Greetings From The

North Missouri Saddle Club Inc.
Trenton, Missouri

1957 Officers: President Leland Duke, Vice-President Darl Doolin, Secretary Mrs Hazel Lowrey. This club participates in parades, trail rides, and all horse show.s in North Central Missouri. All persons interested in horses are cordially invited to take a membership in this club.

BACK ROW: Clarence McCollum, Bobby Vanderpool, Melvin Kackley (Clerks), Ernest Rumbley (Assistant Manager), -Boyd "Buck" McCaslin (Meat Department Head), J. B. Fisk (Butch if) and Roger Blackburn (Manager). FRONT ROW: Doris Spradling, Oma Kent (Checkers), Marie McCaslin (Meat Clerk), Elsie Clark (Checker).

CONGRATULATIONS: To survive 100 years, to grow and prosper for a Century, is a feat which anyone maybe proud.

Trenton reached that ten decade milestone this year. As Trenton grew, so did its people, its schools, its businesses, and all the rest that go to make up what we affectionately call our city.

A & P is proud to have contributed to this progress. We have tried to keep pace with the ever increasing demand made upon us by Trenton residents. We progressed here because, Trenton families have come to realize we help bring them quality foods at low prices. In return, they passed through our store in greater numbers each year.

Today, A & P looks forward to the birth of Trenton's second century, determined to serve the next generation of residents , with the same efficiency that made their mothers and fathers, grandmothers and grandfathers our friends.

The Great Atlantic & Pacific Tea Co.

Meeting The Trains WAS MORE LEISURELY IN THE GOOD OLD DAYS.

Charley Dye who drove the mail wagon is holding up several letters and is surrounded by: Left to Right: Ernest Dye, standing on ground, Russell Hatfield, R. Kelly, Burl Murphy, and Tommy Hughes.

Mary Moore, Hattie Dragoo, Louise Crawford, Luetta Wilford, Beverly Swank, Florence Stafford, Edna Snyder, C. D. Garlich s .

Joe's Sandwich Shop & Restaurant

The Best And Most Complete Eating Establishment In Trenton
Courteous Service - Good Food - Pleasant Atmosphere
Breakfasts - Plate Lunches - Dinners - Steaks - Short Orders
Sandwiches - Fountain Service - Catering Service

TOP PICTURE: Left to Right: Our Delivery Fleet and Salesmen; Roy Shockey, Jud Shockey, George Giles, Richard Price, Melvin Sharp, Don Sheppard, Marvin Good. MIDDLE PICTURE: Todays Production Line and Employees, Left to Right: Ronald Talley, Franklin Layson, Louis Allnutt, W. T. Figgins, Frank Davis, David Booth, jud Shockey, Roy Shockey, Marvin Good, Dorothy Huff, Bookkeeper; Tad A. Simons, Manager. LOWER PICTURE: Taken around 1900, first bottle washer and delivery wagon.

Bottled Coca-Cola through more than half a century in the same location. Founded by Geo. B. Simons in 1897, Second Bottler of Coca-Cola west of the Mississippi. Now owned and managed by his son, Tad A. Simons.

TRENTON COCA-COLA CO.

Old water works was in the bottom land below the present location.

Old Water Works Engine House

The present manager of the Trenton Utilities is Lester Kempton. Chairman of the Board of Public Works is Ray V. Denslow. Board members are: Dr. C. H. Cullers, Charles Skinner, Edwin Knudsen.

Grand River Lodge No. 52

The I.O.O.F. Grand River Lodge #52 was founded in 1852. The officers for 1957 are as follows: Noble Grand, Ed Carter; Vice-Grand, Hurless Wyatt; Recording Secretary, J. S. Wilson; Financial Secretary, George Ritko; Treasurer, Oka Moss; Warden, Ralph Lankford; Conductor, Bob Spickard; Chaplain, C. H. Adams; R.S. to N.G. , K. B. Conrad, L.S. to N.G. , Grover Brown; R.S. to V.G., William Kindred; L.S. to V.G., James Clevenger; Inside Guardian, Harry McKay; Outside Guardian, George Mapes; Acting P.N.G., Cecil Ellis; Right Scene Supporter, W. O. Abernathy; Left Scene Supporter, B. F. Porter.

The Staff of the Davis-Blackmore Funeral Home is proud to participate in Trenton's Centennial Celebration.

We are proud of our town, our county, and our trade territory.

By progressive thought and action, let's make it an even better place in which to live in the years that lie ahead.

"AVAILABLE TO ALL REGARDLESS OF FINANCIAL CONDITION"

SEATED: Gordon Blackmore, Mrs. Helen Fordyce.
STANDING: Claude Crandall, Fred Doty, Harold Roberts.

DAVIS-BLACKMORE FUNERAL HOME

PHONE 232   TRENTON, MISSOURI   813 CUSTER

The Trenton Fire Department

The Trenton Fire Company was organized in Trenton, April 2, 1873, with thirty-eight members and called the "Trenton Fire King". In June of the same year the organization had sixty members on the roll, the limit being eighty. The reason for so many members was necessitated by the "Bucket Brigade" method of fire fighting.

The Fire King became defunct and was "forced to abdicate", but a new company soon took its place, being organized under the city charter, July 2, 1889, and for many years known as the "Rough and Ready Fire Company". The equipment of the company consisted of a hook and ladder wagon and two hose carts. The membership was limited to fifty, with thirty actual fire fighters, inferring that it was a more exclusive organization than its predecessor. Actually fewer men were needed, because in 1886 a water works was established with fire hydrants in the city, enabling the hose cart crews to replace the Bucket Brigade.

WILEY ESTES
Retired Fire Chief
Age 87

The old hose cart was at first composed of a pair of six foot wheels on an axle supporting a hose reel. A long rope was attached to the tongue with sufficient length for a dozen men to grab hold and run with the apparatus, while two men held up the weight of the tongue and helped guide the cart. Later, the tongue was taken off, shafts taking its place, and the apparatus was pulled by a horse.

After "Old Prince", the fire horse, died in 1916, a new 40-horsepower Buckeye, chain-driven motor fire wagon was purchased. The purchase was not made until after a hose was placed in the old well at five points and the new motor forced up a stream of water almost as high as the flag pole.

In 1918, after two years of service, the Buckeye was traded for a White which was used for more than 20 years.

In 1891, Garrett Heinen became Trenton's Fire Chief. He served until 1917 when Wiley Estes was appointed to fill his place. Estes, who started on the Fire Department in 1888, when he was 18 years old, served a total of 51 years before retiring in 1939.

C. E. (Hook) Estes, became the Fire Chief upon the retirement of his father, Wiley Estes. Other Fire Chiefs have been Hobart Sparks, R. R. (Rusty) Vance, Archie Somerville and Hobart Sparks, present Fire Chief.

Employed at present are four regular firemen and twelve volunteers. Several of the volunteers have served a number of years. Ray Van Meter holds the record with 30 years as a volunteer fire fighter.

BACK ROW: Left to Right: Harold Brown, Lyle Kirk, Charles Powell, Cecil Cisco. FRONT ROW: Carolyn Asman, Dorthy Eicher, Pauline Snyder, Donna McNabb.

For nearly three quarters of the Centennial year there has been a drug store in continuous operation at our location. First opened in 1876 by Dr. Kimblin, followed in 1905 by Alison Nicholas. The next owner was Edelein who sold the business to O'Fallon in 1914. Successive operators have been Lafferty Shirley 1919, Bedford 1922, Cisco 1930 and the Centennial owners Cecil Cisco and Harold Brown who formed the partnership in 1950.

CISCO-BROWN DRUG STORE

Prescription Specialists

Country Club

One cold night in March, 1908, about eight men were to be found sitting in McGuire's Drug Store talking of the things which men are wont to talk of. Among the group was James A. Perry, world traveler and journalist, who had worked for the New York Times and Kansas City Star, but at that time was employed by the Republican-a veritable Colonel Mulberry Sellers.

The trend of the conversation turned to golf, and B. J. McGuire remarked that he had never seen the game played. Perry, on the other hand was quite proficient in the game and had played in both. America and Europe. As the conversation grew more and more interesting, someone asked why Trenton couldn't have a golf course. Perry said it could, and offered to pick out the ground. The next day was Sunday, and a delegation headed by Perry were out bright and early looking for golf course sites. Several locations were visited, but none pleased the only golfer in the crowd, and finally in desperation, Mr. McGuire suggested a place where he once drove cows, and standing waist deep in buck brush, while holding onto a sapling to keep from falling into a ravine, Mr. Perry declared it a perfect site for a golf course.

Twenty-three acres were rented from J. R. Wright, and it was suggested that Perry lay out the course; he declined, suggesting that a professional be hired for the job, but the men insisted that he knew as much about it as a professional, so he finally consented. In the first shipment of equipment which Perry ordered, came the metal plates that sat flush with the ground. to mark the forward position of the ball. Perry insisted that these were to tee the ball off on-all the wooden clubs were broken the first week! Prior to the construction of the course, Mr. Perry held a school of instruction in Winter's Hall. And so Trenton had one of the earliest golf courses in Missouri outside of the large cities.

The club house, rustic in style, was built in 1908 and added to from time to time. In 1914, the club bought seventy-five acres from A. G. Knight. The present nine-hole golf course was constructed in 1921.

Berts Shoe Shop

Shoe Repairing and Build Ups
"Everything For The Shoe But The Foot".

Owner and Operator For The Past Eight Years.
Your Patronage Appreciated
Bert and Dorthea Hudson

Inez Bender, Waldo Bender,
Alma Laundy, Edna Browning

BEER and SANDWICHES

Trenton Tavern

803 Main Street

Bullock Jewelry

903 Main

Our 10th Year

Opened as a watch repair shop in 1947 at 1002 Tinsman, in 1952 moving to 811 Washington in the Hyde Building and adding a line of jewelry, continuing in that location until 1956 when our store was moved to our present location and expanded our lines of jewelry, watches, clocks, watch and jewelry repairing to better serve our customers.

Bob and Marge Bullock

Owned and operated by Bob and Mary Ellis for the last eleven years.

903 Main
Phone 163

400 E. 4th
Phone 1728

"We Grow Our Own"

Ellis Flowers and Greenhouses

Five Points In The Ninties MANY CHANGES HAVE BEEN MADE.
DO YOU RECOGNIZE ANY OF THE BUILDINGS?

Tripp Vault

2109 E. 10th St.

Automatic Music Co.

Coin Operated
Phonographs and Games
320 West 10th St. - Phone 122

Bill Welch – Art Hunolt

Trenton, Mo.

The Early Taxis WERE A BIT SLOW, BUT QUITE ELEGANT.

The driver is Russel Hatfield. His team was Charley (in front) and Buck. They met all of the passenger trains.

Gardner-Flesher Coal Co.

1920   1957

Another Leading Grocery AT THE TURN OF THE CENTURY WAS RATLIFF & SCOTT BROS. IT WAS LOCATED ON MAIN ST., TWO DOORS NORTH OF FAIR DRUG STORE

LEFT to RIGHT: John Procter, Laura Dennis, Harley Gallatin, Kemp Scott, Unknown, Lee Ratliff and Everett Shields.

Mary's Cafe

Home Cooked Meals & Pies

Highway 65 Cutoff

Trenton, Missouri

Martin-Casebeer Insurance Agency

INSURANCE,
    LOANS,
        SURETY BONDS

Lillie Martin - Gladys Casebeer

104 1/2 East 9th St.

Trenton, Mo.

The Old Water Tower

The old tower stood as a landmark since 1887. It was 130 feet high, fifteen feet in diameter with a capacity of 175,000 gallons. The new tank built in 1936 at a cost of $25,000. It has a capacity of 300,000 gallons.

(Continued From Page 60)

came here under instructions from Grand Commander S. A. Gilbert and set the new comma niery at work under charter which had been ordered and dated October 26, 1874.

CENTENNLAL OFFICERS ARE: Trenton Lodge No. 111: Earl Ebbe, Master; IomerMullins, Senior Warden; (Junior Warden, Vacant). Trenton Chapter 66 R. A. M: Fred Asman, High Priest; Eric Sonnich, King; Homer Mullins, Scribe. Trenton Council No. 37: Frank Kercheval, Illustrious Master; W. R. Robbins, Deputy Master; Jerrold Stuart, C.C.; Godfrey de Bouillon Commandery; Dr. Edward Nixon, Commander; Frank Kercheval, Generalissimo; Hugh Graham, Captain General.

L to R: Seth Griffin, Chase Williams, Ruth Spencer, Walter Spencer.

Spencer Hatchery & Produce Co.

Quisenberry and Dannen Feeds

Hy 65 North   Phone 1608

Huffstutter & Newton Body Shop

All Kinds of Body Work

Auto Glass Installed

Fast, Economical & Dependable Service

Jewett Norris Public Library

„public library was not secured until 1890, when Jewett Norris, cne of the early pioneers and leading citizens of Grundy county gave the city a gift of $50,000 to be used in constructing a public library. Norris, who had lived most of his life in Grundy county, moved to St. Paul, Minn., in the declining years of his life, but his heart and interests remained with his old friends and comrades in Trenton. When he left for his new home in the north, he estimated that he had earned $50,000 while a resident of this county, and by wise investment of this capital he was able to enlarge this amount severalfold. Feeling that Grundy county and its residents were the ones responsible for his good fortune, he saw fit to return the original sum to the community in a way by which all could share alike. The library was an institution which was badly needed.

WESTERN AUTO ASSOCIATE STORE
Home Owned by, Ernie Rousselot

The Family Store
Featuring Merchandise
Designed For Today's Living
At Yesterday's Prices

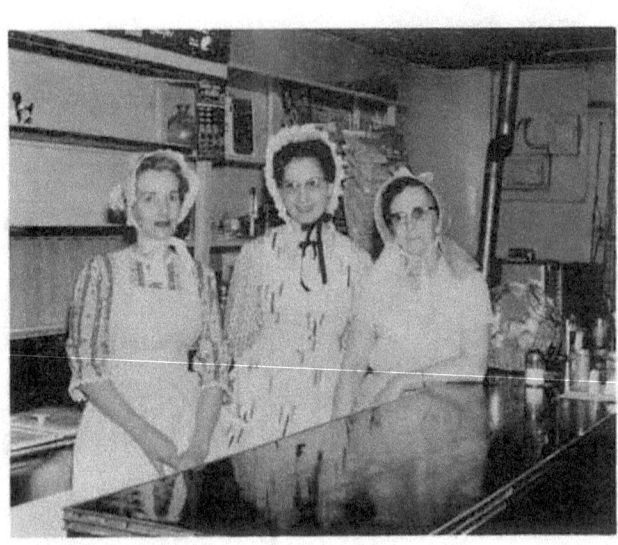

Hickman Tripp Inn

Meals Served Daily

Pyatt Insurance Agency

Best Wishes For The Success Of
OUR CENTENNIAL
All Kinds of Stock Company
INSURANCE
We Have Been in Business Here
26 Years

Looking South ON WHAT IS NOW MAIN STREET, TOWARDS FIVE POINTS SIXTY YEARS AGO.

May's D-X Service

For Tank Wagon Service
Ray Coon - Phone 1769
Laredo Phone ATlas 6-3197
Tank Wagon Service

Serving Trenton 22 Years

Zenith Radio and TV
Carrier Heating and Air Conditioning
Kelvinator

Peery Electric Shop

Scene at Collier Springs, July 12, 1893

BACK ROW: Left to Right: Rupert Conrads, Harry Lanius, Nellie Carnes (Kircher), Nellie Lowen (Merrill), Ralph Conrads. SECOND ROW: Ethel Shanklin (Brown), Mildred Phillips (Iiausam), Kathryn Raffauf. FIRST ROW: Flora Dutcher, Katie Conrads (Wolz), Anna Fulkerson (Smith), Letha Lowen, Carrie Walker.

Young people enjoyed an outing much as we do today. This group met at Collier Springs (just south of the bridge at Charley Dye's). They belonged to a club and the girls made their own hats which were of brown straw and brown material. They are all alike except for two.

Early Hotel

One of the earliest hotels, or taverns, as they were called in the early days, was Tracy's Tavern, managed by James B. Tracy. Its location was in a block south of the present courthouse. Besides filling the need of a lodging house for travelers, it was the meeting place for the townspeople, much as the drug store is at the present day. It was in this tavern that the Trenton lodges of Masons and Oddfellows were organized, maintaining rooms there several months. How long this tavern was in existence is not known, but of a certainty it existed in 1849.

RICE IN GRUNDY COUNTY

An attempt to raise rice in Grundy county was made in 1925-26 by A.G. Knight in the American Bottoms south of Trenton. The 160 acres which were planted were kept under water by a pump supplying water from the river. The first year enough rice was raised to seed the land the following year. The project was given up because of the short growing seasons of this country which would not give the rice a chance to mature.

CENTENNIAL GREETINGS

FROM

Trenton Diner

Interior Of

Bill Crook's Grocery

He Handled A Large Variety Of "Staples And Fancy Groceries"

CENTENNIAL GREETINGS
From

Whitley Popcorn Co.

Trenton, Missouri

Katherine Miller, Opal, Henry, Beverly Goodin, "Pete" Spencer.

Thanks To Everyone Who Has Helped To Make Our 10 Years In Business A Success.

Goodin Cleaners

Old Time Banks WERE SIMPLE AND COMPACT

The Farmers and Merchants Bank, founded in 1894. C. P. Brandom was president; Geo. Wolz, vice-president and W. P. Fulkerson, cashier. (Jim Collier reports that this bank was located where Bonta and Noel now have their barber shop).

BACK ROW: Tayler French, Clifford Arbuckle, Mrs. Laura Roberts, Marion Smith, Marie Halfield, Deana Roberts, Nina Roberts, Donna Roberts, Harry Barnes, Harry McKay, Ernie Dye. FRONT ROW: James Bryant, Donald Roberts, Howard Hobbs, Lawrence French.

Roberts Cab Co.
DURING THE NEXT 100 YEARS RIDE WITH ROBERTS CABS
PHONE 203

www.ingramcontent.com/pod-product-compliance
Lightning Source LLC
Chambersburg PA
CBHW081233170426
43198CB00017B/2753